"Little Robot, Big Dreams"

The Highs, Lows, & Lessons Learned of a SharkTank Startup

by Jeremy Scheinberg & Chris Harden

This book is dedicated to Laurie, Rachel, Sophia, Jacob, and Asher. We could not have taken this journey without your love and support.

Table of Contents:

By the Skin of Our Teeth

11:40 PM…

We were 20 minutes away from the end of our Kickstarter campaign. There we sat, in our co-working space in downtown Orlando, staring at our computer screens, delirious and giddy with fatigue. It had been an intense three months leading up to the end of this cannonball run, and an exhausting nine months since we committed to start TROBO. Now, it was down to the wire. Twenty minutes to reach our funding goal or get nothing. There was no in-between; we would either raise enough money or our business would die.

And the clock kept ticking…

11:40PM

11:41PM

…

Preface

How This Book is Setup

This book details our timeline, our emotional journey, and some lessons learned as we joined forces to create the world's first storytelling robot. Throughout our careers, we have both read plenty of business books but one thing that was constantly missing was a book that really detailed the entrepreneurs' journey and emotions. "Entrepreneurs" is plural because that is the other difference between this book and others. Most books that we have read are told from one person's perspective. Building a company by yourself is impossible. Even if there is one prominent person who is the face of the company, there are always other people behind the scenes that are responsible for the company's success. We are a team. We both bring different skills to the table and that comes through in the TROBO journey. When writing this book, we have each written various sections and then edited each other to bring in both voices. In that way, this is a unique book and really pays tribute to the fact that it takes a village to raise a robot.

As Entrepreneurs, we have enjoyed the gambit of emotions and steep learning curves. If you are reading this, you are probably interested in that part of our experience the most, so we'll share our...

Emotions: (what we were feeling at that moment)
Lesson(s) Learned: (the good, the bad, the furry)

A Note on Fear

As we were writing this book and detailing our emotions, one feeling kept coming back over and over again. That feeling was fear. In our case, it is a completely rational fear. It is perfectly normal to be afraid when you have quit your jobs to pursue the unknown. But fear kept creeping into our lives at every step of the way. When you have taken such a big risk, you can feel that every decision – no matter how minor it may seem – could be the one that dooms your new business. Whether it is a big decision – like choosing your corporate entity type – or a seemingly little one – what type of shirts to order – no decision seems insignificant when you are in the trenches. So fear factors in to every one of those decisions and it often prevents you from making a choice. As we grew with the company, the one thing we were constantly reminded of is that it is better to make a decision and move on, than to let fear slow us down. It's not always easy to do this, but we know indecision is a momentum killer.

So just because fear may be missing from our emotions as we tell our story doesn't mean it wasn't there. We took big risks and it's OK for us to have been at least a little afraid. Hopefully, you can learn from our fear and keep on moving.

One Comment Before We Begin…

This book details a work in progress. We would love to tell you that when you reach the end, you will hear how we reached financial freedom, got TROBOs into the hands of millions of children and made TROBO a household name. That's a great dream but – as we are writing this – it just doesn't exist. By the time you read this, we may be fulfilling that dream or we may be reflecting on what might have been. We may be continuing to hustle or we may be working on our next big thing. Either way, we have learned so much from this journey and hope we can share those insights with someone who can benefit from them. You never know – one piece of information in this book may be all that separates you from your dream.

For now, there is no better place to start then at the beginning…

Background: Our Brief Histories and How We Met

Jeremy grew up in Miami. From the time he was a little kid, he always knew he wanted to be an engineer. He was constantly curious about how things worked. Jeremy loved to visit Disney World but he looked at the parks from a different perspective; rather than "watching the show", Jeremy always tried to peek behind the scenes to learn how the rides worked – what's a sensor? What does that big button do? Those trips inspired him to want to work as a theme park engineer.

He attended the University of Pennsylvania where he studied Systems Engineering. The summer before his senior year, he worked as an intern in the Engineering department at Disney World. While it was an incredible experience, a hiring freeze meant that Disney wasn't going to be an option. However, his experience at Disney allowed him to discover Alcorn McBride – the company that built audio, video and control equipment for theme parks and museums all over the world. A few months after graduating, Jeremy started with Alcorn as an engineer. He would help with product design and – every spring – he would travel around the world working on new projects for companies including Disney, Universal and Lego.

Jeremy's wife Rachel had come to Orlando and made some career sacrifices to help Jeremy pursue his dream so when the time came for Rachel to pursue her career, Jeremy and Rachel moved to Minnesota. While Rachel worked, Jeremy went back to school to get his MBA. Although they had a great experience in Minnesota, Rachel missed the palm trees and warmth of Orlando so they decided to return. Jeremy returned to Alcorn McBride as Chief Operating Officer and was thrilled to be working alongside his friends and teammates. Working at Alcorn was an amazing experience full of great people, endless design challenges and a supportive team. But Jeremy had gotten a little restless and missed being an engineer. He had never started a venture of his own, as he was pretty risk-averse but he wondered if maybe it was time for something different. Jeremy and Rachel now had two amazing kids – Sophia (age 5) and Jacob (age 2) – and the stress of work was starting to get to him. While Alcorn was an amazing place to work – and was very family friendly – he was constantly taking his work stress home and he was worried that it was affecting his relationship with his family. By the fall of 2013, Jeremy began to get the entrepreneurial itch.

Chris grew up mostly in Alabama. He lived in more of a gypsy style family and moved a lot as a child. Early on he found he had a knack for school, and eventually went to the Alabama School of Math and Science. That led to Auburn University, where he began in Industrial Design, and eventually found his calling in Electrical Engineering. Unlike Jeremy, who had such intense focus on his goal career since he was a child, Chris hadn't heard of what engineering was until he attended Auburn. In his senior project, he became friends with Jason Crew, who told him about the thriving theme park industry in Orlando. Chris was star struck and a year later Chris leapt at the chance to join Alcorn McBride and the exciting theme park industry. He joined Jason, Jeremy, Steve Alcorn (the company's Founder), and a crew of extremely talented engineers and staff. Six years later, Laurie, Chris's wife, pursued her lifelong dream of going to medical school, and they left Orlando. They moved to Tampa, and while there Chris worked full time, got his MBA, and worked as an illustrator and inker for small press and major comic book publishers, getting to work on titles like Spiderman, Batman, Tomb Raider, Witchblade, and The Darkness, to name a few.

He spent the next six years of his career at a consulting company called BSQUARE, where he was one of the Tech Leads on the Coca Cola Freestyle UI, the Ford My Touch UI, and the Kindle Fire. During his time in Tampa, Chris cofounded his first startup Personal Memory Systems, landing seed investment to explore the concept of 24/7 recording of all audio and video memories a person experiences. Later he created Phone-Tag, a scavenger hunt mobile phone game on Windows Mobile Phones. His third venture was a graphic novel called "The Fro" that Chris promoted by dressing up as the character at local conventions and performing in the US Air Guitar circuit, landing 5th place nationwide in 2009. With each concept Chris learned more about what *not* to do with a startup.

When Laurie finished Residency, Chris left engineering to become a film student in the MFA program at Florida State University, a school widely regarded as the 5th best film school in the country. After about a year, and after the birth of his beautiful boy, Asher, Chris recognized he could not be a great father and a great filmmaker, so he left the school and headed back to his favorite town, Orlando. Chris knew he wanted to start another business, and by now he knew he needed people he could trust. He thought about his networks in Alabama, Seattle, and Orlando. Seattle was just too expensive, Alabama was not really strong, but Orlando was just right. He and Laurie wanted to raise Asher in the entertainment capital of the world, and Chris knew his network was strong with tech guys from Alcorn and artists from his comic book days. Jeremy didn't know it, but Chris considered him to be one of the best candidates in his network, who'd make a stellar partner.

Chris knew Electronic Arts was in town, so he applied. He became a Development Director, and enjoyed two years of game development at one of the best studios in the world. He managed central teams that developed core libraries used by all the major sports games produced by EA – Madden, FIFA, UFC, NHL, Tiger Woods, etc.… Then Startup Weekend happened, and that's where the TROBO story begins.

Year 1: Launch, Prototype, Kickstart!

One Crazy Weekend & the Beginning of an Idea

TROBO was born one long weekend in Orlando in November, 2013. But it wasn't just any weekend. TROBO was born at an event called Startup Weekend. Equal parts inspiration, collaboration and exhaustion, Startup Weekend is a place where ideas come to thrive or die.

Startup Weekend was a great way to tiptoe into entrepreneurship; there is no commitment beyond a weekend of your time. The structure worked like this:
You go in on Friday night and anyone who wants to pitch an idea does a quick pitch in front of the group. One minute, no PowerPoint or Keynote slides - just a quick pitch.
The group votes on which ideas they like the best and then you form teams around the top ideas. The rest of the ideas….Well, maybe those get saved for another day, or congratulations – you just failed fast!

Over the course of the weekend, the emphasis was on validation – get your idea in front of as many people as possible and see if your idea had legs. If it doesn't, fail and join another team.
If your idea did have legs, see how far you could take it. In the best case, you could try to get people to pay for it. If not, see if you could get some kind of commitment from people.
Sunday night was pitch night. Present your idea in front of the group and a team of judges and may the best business win.

Chris and Jeremy both pitched their ideas on Friday night. Chris's idea was for a mobile app. Jeremy's idea was for a plastic talking robot that would help young children to learn about programming. After the voting process, Jeremy tried to form a team. People kept coming up to Jeremy and saying what a great idea it was. But when people declared their allegiance to a team, all of those people who had declared their love for the robot project, joined other teams. Reflecting back on that time, it seemed like people didn't choose the robot project because they wanted to win the weekend. It's important to know that there were no giant trophies or enormous checks for winning Startup Weekend. But people decided that hardware was difficult; all of the other teams were developing apps and while it was conceivable to develop an app by the end of the weekend, it was obvious that we wouldn't be developing a functional robot prototype in a day and a half. One of those people who did see the potential was Chris, who - thanks to an incredible skillset and a previous working relationship with Jeremy - helped launch TROBO on the right foot at that Weekend. Thankfully, we did have some courageous people who joined our team and we started to move forward with the concept.

On the original Team TROBO were Carlos, Michael, Jean, David, Jeremy, and Chris. Everyone came to the meetings, and everyone worked hard. We made a great Startup Weekend team.

We were excited about the possibility of a toy that could get kids excited about science, technology, engineering and math (STEM). But as we talked about it, we thought about the manufacturing challenges that would lie ahead. More importantly, we thought about how much money it would take to build it. Anything that required plastic needed expensive tooling and we looked at the problem and said "How would we be able to raise the millions of dollars to bring this to market?" Rather than give up, we went back to our mission. If the overall idea was good, how could we modify the concept to make it buildable? Chris suggested a plush toy with a Bluetooth speaker as the MVP, instead of a plastic toy, so we pivoted on hardware. In addition, we chose to create a robot that told stories instead of one that taught programming, which was good, since we later learned there seemed to be a hundred robots and games that teach children to program. We also hatched the critical idea of including the child in the story that weekend, but it was going to be a cropped photo of the child. Later we changed it to a cartoon drawing. We did some sketches and refined the concept and then we went outside to interview people get some feedback. We got some great stories and people seemed to like our idea. We tested pricing and continued to refine the idea over the weekend.

People often ask where the name comes from. We white-boarded a few names, like SBOT, TROBO, TROBOT, and others, and TROBO just seemed to have a nice ring to it. Unfortunately not a clever story there, but who says a bit of dumb luck is a bad thing every once in a while?

But if we wanted to have the strongest idea, we knew we needed to build a TROBO. We went to a fabric store and – while other teams were coding and building their apps – we sewed! We built an adorable – though slightly awkward – plush toy robot who we affectionately refer to now as "Grandpa TROBO."

Figure 1 - Grandpa TROBO and "TROBO's Escape From Venus", our Startup Weekend MVP

By Sunday night, we had Grandpa TROBO (no Bluetooth connection) and a series of full screen mockups using mostly off-the-shelf graphic art, showing one flow of a child going on a digital adventure with TROBO, helping him fix his broken rocket ship and get back to Earth. We used the photo browser app to simulate the flows, because at that point no one on the team had built iOS apps before.

We got to Sunday's pitch event and put together the strongest presentation we could. But in the end, the star of the show was Grandpa TROBO. We tailored our presentation by leading with the problem that we saw with our own kids. Their curiosity about science and our inability as parents to find an alternative to mindless toys and apps to help inspire our kids, resonated with the judges (who were also parents and grandparents). As we listened to the other teams present, we didn't feel great about our chances.

After the presentations, they called several teams up to the front including us and we felt like we were in one of those "If you are standing up here, thanks for playing but you did not win." It wasn't until they started awarding those teams 5th place, 4th place, etc. that we started to get excited. When they announced that TROBO had won 2nd place, we were ecstatic! It had been a phenomenal experience and to get some recognition – even 2nd place – made us feel great.

Despite different skills, Chris and Jeremy had something important in common – family. Both had small children at home and saw the curiosity that lives inside them. Jeremy's 5 year old daughter, Sophia was constantly asking questions about the world around her but the toys and apps she played with did nothing to answer her questions. Asher, Chris's son was playing way too much with cars instead of educational toys. When Chris and Jeremy relayed their experiences at home and their frustrations with mindless toys and apps, they realized that maybe they weren't alone. Maybe other parents felt the same way?

Startup Weekend was a great way to get our idea out there and to test it but – like many ideas that were hatched at Startup Weekend – we figured TROBO would end there. The team members went their separate ways, but Jeremy and Chris had worked together before and – as we followed up with each other – we started to think that maybe TROBO had some real potential.

Emotions: Excitement, curiosity

Lesson(s) Learned: Look for opportunities to test your ideas. Don't assume that just because no one else is doing it doesn't mean that your idea has no merit. Test it out.

Jumping into the Startup Pool

After the elation of Startup Weekend, many of the businesses "die on the vine." However, we continued to think of TROBO and wonder about its possibilities. Jeremy had started to do teach-ins at local elementary schools – using theme parks as a canvas to get kids excited about engineering careers. After discussing it with his wife and with the support of Steve Alcorn, Jeremy decided to leave Alcorn McBride to work on TROBO full-time in January. At the time Chris was managing the IGNITE UI group at EA. With Laurie's support, Chris booked his evenings and weekends on TROBO. Chris would join fulltime on July 4th as the Kickstarter campaign began to take shape.

While Jeremy focused on finding money, manufacturers, and anyone who could help guide us, Chris focused on plush and app prototyping, TROBO's first story contest, etc. Our early conversations circled around funding with Kickstarter, so we set out building our core network of supporters. We built our Parental Focus group, a set of 60 friends and family who were moms, dads, grandmothers, grandfathers, etc. who had children in the target age range for TROBO. In the early days, they were the sounding board for everything TROBO. We put them in a SurveyMonkey list, and about once a month, we sent out surveys.

Driven by Design

TROBO's development is based on traditional Industrial Design principals. The basics are "go wide with many concepts, and based on regular customer and design reviews, narrow in on the most popular and appropriate design." The TROBO plush started out as about 20 sketches of wildly different shapes and sizes, square, triangular, muscular, pear-shaped, etc.… We voted those down to 5 or so and then put them in front of the Parental Focus Group. Once the basic physical shape was chosen (a pear belly shape), we brainstormed about 20 different chest logos, all related to someone successful in their chosen field of study, narrowed those down, and let our focus group pick the winner. In the early days, we were exploring names such as Newton, Edison, Carver, Tyco, Tesla, Curie, Ada, etc....

For color schemes we started out with one color scheme that was neutral to boys and girls. We didn't receive good reviews on this and decided to launch with two SKUs – one for boys and one for girls. We used basic color theory of quads and triads settling on a handful of three for each gender. The parental focus group helped us pick Edison's first, and later they helped us pick the scheme for Curie.

For the mobile app, we sketched several art styles and asked the parents to choose the one they think looked the most compelling for TROBO. Chris will admit his favorite art style for the app was not picked, nor were his favorite set of plush colors for the Curie toy. But when you are crowd-driven, building a product for the market, you gotta go with what people tell you they like the most. Otherwise, there is no point in asking.

Emotions: Fun. Creating your early products is nothing but fun.

Lessons Learned: Don't be afraid to get feedback on your product from day 1. You'll make a better product for exposing it early. Also your early participants will be your biggest help, when you try to Kickstart or sell later, because they are invested in you from day 1.

Our First Trip to Toy Fair
In February of 2014, Jeremy made his first trip to Toy Fair. Part research trip, part "Bucket List" item, the New York International Toy Fair is one of the largest toy conventions in the world. It takes place every February at the Javits Convention Center in New York City and it is the place where toy manufacturers – big and small – show off their latest wares to retailers (also big and small). It's also a high profile event where the press looks for what is going to be the "Hot New Toy for the Holiday Season." Yes, we did say the holiday season...in February. But the reality is – as we would soon learn – that the holiday season starts even earlier.

Jeremy's trip to Toy Fair aimed to accomplish three things: get a quick education on the toy industry, find a potential prototyping partner for the plush toy and – most of all – to see if it was even remotely realistic for two guys in a garage to build a toy company.

The introduction to the toy industry looked to be a difficult proposition. While it was easy to walk the aisles and see how toy manufacturers positioned their products, just learning how they got those products into stores seemed daunting. There were just so many toys there! And while there was the occasional "Why would any kid ever want to play with that?" most of the toys were awesome. The reality is that stores – both the big retailers like Target, Wal-Mart and Toys R Us and smaller "mom and pop" toy stores – have limited shelf space. They want to occupy that shelf space with winners – sure things and they don't like to take risks. That means that it is easier for them to buy the next Barbie than it is to buy TROBO. The other thing we learned is that marketing is king. A big company like Mattel can spend millions of dollars on TV advertising as well as TV shows and movies that can get kids excited about their latest toy. Our reality is that those kinds of venues would never be accessible to us, given our limited means.

But we also learned that the landscape was changing in a couple of different ways. First, marketing was changing. Parents didn't just look at traditional marketing channels – TV, newspaper, magazine advertising – to find cool new toys. Marketing was evolving more towards social channels – Facebook, Twitter, Pinterest – as well as heavily listening to their favorite "Mommy Blogger" (or "Daddy Blogger"). Parents have created businesses of their own by reviewing and promoting new products and they have very loud and influential voices. Some parent bloggers charge for that influence (and it can be very expensive). Others want to be on the bleeding edge of new products and they want to find the coolest toys for their own kids (and for other kids). The result is that this can help give voice to the little guy- a new toy company (like TROBO) that would never have the ability to compete with the big guy (if you are active and do things the right way).

The other thing we learned at Toy Fair was how the retail landscape was changing. Everywhere at the Fair, people were talking about the power of Amazon. It was no secret how big Amazon was but people were talking more and more about the power of "Showrooming." In short, "Showrooming" is when a potential customer walks into a "brick and mortar" store – like a Best Buy or small independent toy retailer – to get an idea of what toys are out there (or to check out something specific). They are able to hold the product in their hands – and then they whip out their smartphone and order it on Amazon. With Amazon Prime's free 2-day shipping, unless they need that product right there and then, they will go for the lower price. This creates a tipping point for a new toy company; while it's important to be in brick and mortar stores so your product can be visible, how many toys are you actually going to sell through those channels? At Toy Fair, we kept hearing that traditional retail channels, especially smaller "mom and pop" stores, were becoming less important from a volume perspective. But we also heard that these retailers were willing to take more chances and showing off cool new products that bigger retailers wouldn't. They wouldn't be ordering hundreds of units at a time but they would put your product on the shelf and – if it sold well – this could attract attention from the big boys.

The other thing we learned about the industry is timing. While we had previously heard that all the big retailers made their decisions at Toy Fair, we learned that if you wanted to be in stores for the holidays, they needed you to have the toys ready to ship to their warehouses by June! That's right, June! We didn't yet know how this would impact us but it was definitely an important fact to consider. It wasn't until our second Toy Fair that we would learn even more about the holiday schedule.

We were fortunate enough to learn a lot about the industry from some great people. Some were willing to answer our questions and help out a new company while some told us to "buzz off." But our biggest win was finding a manufacturing partner. We knew we would need to build prototypes and then we would do our crowdfunding campaign but finding a manufacturer was proving to be difficult. As Jeremy walked around Toy Fair, meeting plush toy manufacturers, he asked them if they would be willing to do multiple rounds of prototyping – knowing that it would take a couple of rounds to get TROBO just right. Every manufacturer said they would do one round of prototyping and then they expected you to go right into full production. We knew this would not be realistic; the crowdfunding campaign would be launched for a while and then we wouldn't be delivering until even later. We needed someone who would work with us. After speaking with at least 10 manufacturers, we met John. John said he had worked with crowdfunded companies in the past and would be happy to do multiple rounds of prototypes for us. Not only that, but the rough pricing he gave us was much more affordable than that of any of the other – less flexible – manufacturers we met. They had some samples of the work that they had done for major brands and it all looked great. We felt like we had a good lead on a manufacturing partner that could help us put out great looking products and who would work with us to grow.

Our final Toy Fair question – whether two guys in a garage could launch a new toy company – that was a little harder to answer. We looked for other companies that were doing something similar to what we were doing – a connected plush toy with an app – but there didn't seem to be anyone doing that yet. We were fortunate enough to be able to attend the Digital Kids Expo – a conference on emerging trends in app and content products for kids that was held at the Toy Fair. We met some great people and learned about what was happening in the space (and what was coming soon). We felt that TROBO was unique enough that there might be a chance. We also heard from great new toy entrepreneurs like Debbie Sterling from Goldieblox and Alice Brooks from Roominate who had recently launched their successful STEM toy startups. It was certainly inspirational and made us think that it was possible. But we also learned from Debbie and Alice about the importance of a successful Kickstarter and that it would take a lot of money to get product onto shelves.

While Toy Fair was equal parts daunting and fatiguing, the timing couldn't have been better. We were able to learn a lot about this new industry and to figure out whether or not it was realistic for us to try to bring TROBO to market. It also told us where we needed to concentrate our efforts. Unfortunately, the answer seemed to be everywhere.

Emotions: Overwhelmed, encouraged but with a sense that we were tiny.

Lessons Learned: Before you go too far on your idea, see how much you can learn about the industry. If you have the ability to speak to industry experts or to walk a trade show floor to learn the lay of the land, go for it. It's a great way to figure out whether your idea has potential and/or if you have the ability to access the market. It will also give you a real sense of just what your competition looks like.

The Power of Building a Network

It's important to have friends. When you leave a job to start a new company, it often seems like you are alone. But the reality is you just need to know where to look. There is nothing more important when starting a new company than building a network. You never know what help you are going to need – legal advice, accounting, marketing, manufacturing – and if you are alone, you are in trouble.

We both had very different networks. Chris had his networks from Auburn, USF, and FSU, as well as the software world. Jeremy had networks from Penn and Minnesota as well as the theme park and product design industries. While it is very unusual for two business partners to have networks with very little overlap, we had the benefit of two very distinct networks that could help us build a company and get the knowledge that we lacked.

But unfortunately, those networks wouldn't give us everything that we needed. Even though Chris had started a few businesses on his own, starting a business in Orlando was new for both of us and we had no idea what resources existed in Orlando to help us get TROBO off the ground.

Fortunately, Orlando was changing too. Long reliant on citrus and tourism (you may not have heard but there is a relatively famous cartoon mouse who has a home in Central Florida), Orlando and the surrounding communities had been looking for ways to diversify its economy. Visionary leaders like Orlando Mayor Buddy Dyer and Orange County Mayor Teresa Jacobs wanted to create booming high-tech companies. With a strong, entrepreneurial research university in town – the University of Central Florida – and a strong simulation industry, Central Florida had many of the right pieces in place to build an entrepreneurial economy. But one thing that was missing was a startup veteran to help nurture emerging companies.

Gregg Pollack was a serial entrepreneur. He had formed Envy Labs, a successful online consulting business, and then CodeSchool – an online educational portal that helped people learn new programming skills. As an entrepreneur, Gregg knew the value of having those resources to help a company grow. Gregg had been educated in Silicon Valley and saw the resources that were available there to support emerging companies. But he also saw that those same resources did not exist in Central Florida. Specifically, Orlando did not have an accelerator.

An accelerator is a support tool that provides resources for new companies to get on their feet. While different accelerators provide different support, many provide office space, mentorship and formal education on many of the issues that entrepreneurs are lacking. Some even provide funding in exchange for an equity stake in the company. But more importantly, they provide access to a greater network of mentors and potential investors that a new company would not be able to access on their own.

Gregg set aside some office space at Code School and created Starter Studio, Orlando's first accelerator. After a successful first class that produced 7 new companies, Starter Studio accepted Jeremy and Chris into its second class. TROBO finally had an office (even if we did have to share it). It was so important to be able to work together in an office to move the company forward.

With great guidance from the Starter Studio mentors as well as the camaraderie and support of our fellow "Starters", the experience gave us greater authenticity as a company and as entrepreneurs. It helped to build our brand and further widen our network which would be crucial as we organized and launched our crowdfunding campaign. Starter Studio gave us the tools to build a company. Now, it was up to us to put those tools to work.

Emotions: A Sense of community, Supported

Lesson(s) Learned: Find support – not just financial support. Look for places, people and groups that will help keep you on your journey.

Co-Working: a Cool Place to Call Home

Just after we had finished Starter Studio, and we were still working out of the work space there at Envy Labs, a new co-working space was started. The Canvs co-working space was the brainchild of local entrepreneurs who recognized the importance of co-working facilities in the startup ecosystem. For those unfamiliar with the concept, a co-working facility is an open floor plan environment where individuals and companies work side-by-side. They typically don't require the signing of a lease, giving new companies much-needed flexibility. The most important part is the ability to work with other people. The alternative – working at home or at a Starbucks – can be very insular and that lack of community was one of the things that we missed most about our previous companies. By working at Canvs, TROBO had a place to call home and we had people around us. The greatest part about Canvs was that those people around us were many of the same people that had encouraged us along our startup journey. To be able to work side-by-side with them was incredibly inspiring and they definitely helped to keep us going during the tougher times.

We joined Canvs the month it opened, which proved to be very timely, because like many of the early companies, we got extra PR due to their exposure. This actually was an even better move then we fully understood at the time, because Canvs turned into the entrepreneurial hub of the tech scene for Orlando. Starter Studio ran its third incubation class there. Canvs became a central part of the emerging Orlando tech scene and by being there from the beginning, we were along for the ride (we even got pictures of Orlando Mayor Buddy Dyer holding a TROBO!)

Working spaces can build a sense of loyalty just as if you are working in a big company or working as an employee of a company. About two months ago a stranger came in passing out flyers that were advertising another co-working space that was just down the road and supposedly had a better deal than Canvs. Chris felt insulted that he would walk in and start handing out flyers from the competition, so he went to the front desk. Another Canvs team member from a different company also became angry and found a security guard. The security guard escorted the stranger out and the management of Canvs was notified of the activity. If you care about the people you work with and you care about your location and your environment in many ways working in a coworking space can feel just like working with a company. We might have different directions that we are taking, but we are all working towards a single purpose of building something bigger than ourselves with limited time. Coworking spaces cannot only provide you a place to work but they can also give you many other things that make your little company seem a little bigger.

Emotions: loyalty

Lessons learned: Get out of the house and co-work.

The Early Search for Funding

When starting a new business, money is critical. You always need more money and – looking back – we probably never realized how much money we would need to launch a new toy. But we were also new enough to the startup game in that we didn't know as much as we should have about getting outside money. You will often hear that it's important to bootstrap as much as possible. Bootstrapping means using your own money to finance your business without surrendering equity to outside investors. We were able to finance our company by drawing from our savings and by operating efficiently. We were both fortunate enough to have working spouses to support our families' living expenses. But we also knew that – even if we were ultimately successful with our crowdfunding campaign – we would need more money to get TROBO to market.

Applying to Techstars
Techstars was the first nationwide high-profile incubator to which we applied. We were already in Starter Studio, which was the local incubator in Orlando. However Techstars was one of the rock star incubators that many tech companies want to get into, because of the sheer exposure they gain from being a part of that family. It's a concentrated three-month effort, where the founder or founders go and stay and work on their business plan, network, etc. It's located in several large cities, like New York and Boulder. This Techstars program was even more special as it was a first-time partnership with Disney where 10 companies would work with high-level executives at Disney (including CEO Bob Iger) in addition to getting investment funds. It was just the launch vehicle that we needed.

Like many incubators it had a reasonably lengthy application process, and there are submission videos. There was a team submission video, and a product or service video. Both are less than one minute long. We applied to Techstars in April 2014, which was before we had begun our Kickstarter marketing and video production. So we used the videos that we produced out of our homes.

Chris had a small studio in his house with a white backdrop, some decent video equipment and some photography lights. We were able to produce some reasonably decent product footage for the video. The more interesting part was that we produced our own little music video in a local suburb of Orlando called Winter Park. The video was a parody of Macklemore's wildly successful "Thrift Shop". We called it "Toy Shop" and the premise was that we were trying to raise money by selling all of our old junky toys in to create the new and improved TROBO toy. Jeremy's family came out including his mother-in-law, who is also in the video, his children and wife. They all did a wonderful job. We wrote rap lyrics that communicated our skills, business plan, etc. Since this was an application to the Disney Accelerator, we also referred to Disney in the video. It's still on YouTube if you want to see a good example of what a bad music video looks like. It was a lot of fun, and we believe it is what helped us stand out in the crowd of people who applied to Techstars.

We had a contact there who gave us some insight into the decision process and we apparently got close. But in the end we were not chosen; instead we were invited to apply again next year, once we had made more progress. Anecdotally, we did apply a second time, but we still didn't get in.

Emotions: Fun being ourselves. Disappointment with not getting in.

Lessons Learned: You have to keep trying, and you can't take "no" for an answer. You keep building your product (or service), and even when people don't share in the vision, or at least share in it enough to join you, that doesn't mean they're saying "no." It also doesn't mean that they will always say "no." It means you have yet to show them enough value for them to say yes. So add more value and ask again.

Applying for a Grant

As we mentioned, we were constantly doing demos to validate the TROBO concept and to drum up support for our eventual Kickstarter campaign. But as we showed TROBO to people and demonstrated its potential, we kept hearing from teachers "I wish we had that in my school." Unfortunately, we knew we would have a lot to learn about teachers and schools (as parents we both had exposure to the early learning environment but we knew enough to know we didn't know enough).

It was at this point that we became aware of the Federal government's Small Business Innovation Research (or SBIR) program. Each agency of the Federal government has a portion of their budget allocated by Congress towards funding innovative research by small companies. The SBIR program target "High Risk, High Reward" research opportunities. Different agencies have differing amounts of money to invest in these opportunities but the funds are organized in the form of a multi-phase grant. The Phase I grant is meant to establish "Proof of Feasibility", in other words "will your concept work?" If you are able to prove feasibility, you can apply for the much larger Phase II which focuses on the development and commercialization of the technology. The government does not take equity in your company; in the long run, the hope is that your business will grow, you will hire employees who will pay taxes, your company will pay taxes and those funds that government has invested in you will be reinvested into the economy. It really is an incredible opportunity for companies to perform research and get moving in a way that they might never have the opportunity to do so without the boost.

After attending a seminar on how to apply for an SBIR grant, Jeremy learned that the process was incredibly detailed and involved. The biggest takeaway from the seminar was "If there is a grant opportunity where the deadline is 2 weeks away, don't even bother to try to apply; you will never get it done in time because it takes at least a month to get everything together." With help from Jack Henkel from the Venture Lab at the University of Central

Florida we were able to get our application together for an SBIR grant from the National Science Foundation (NSF). Jack – an early friend of TROBO from the first Startup Weekend – was a tremendous resource and we couldn't have gotten the application together without him.

After 6 months of anxious waiting, we were notified that we had been awarded the grant. The funds gave us the ability to explore new markets for TROBO and – in the end – build a better product.

Emotions: Excitement, anxiety.

Lesson(s) Learned: Keep an eye out for different sources of funding. You never know where support is going to come from.

"We Are Going to Crush You" - The Competition Openly Threatens Us

Entrepreneurial events are a kind of support group for people dipping their toe into the startup pool. They let you know that you are not alone. In addition to continuing to expand your network, they are a great resource to learn from others and share your own learning. But you never know what you are going to learn.

We had been frequent attendees at a local group called One Million Cups, created by the Kauffman Foundation. As Ron Ben Zeev – the local event organizer (a friend we affectionately refer to as the "Godfather of TROBO") – bills it, One Million Cups is "not Shark Tank but, rather "Guppy Tank". It is meant to be a supportive environment where you can present your business and take questions that will help you get an outsider's opinion on your startup in a supportive environment that (hopefully) won't leave you crying in the corner.

So it was with great surprise that Ron came up to Jeremy one Wednesday morning and said "Jeremy, someone wants to meet you." Jeremy followed Ron over to meet this new individual who introduced himself with the words "Hi. We are going to crush you!" After the initial feelings of shock, concern and then anger,

Jeremy got the rest of the story. One of our competitors had been recently accepted into the Techstars Disney Accelerator. It was a tremendous opportunity for them (and one that we desperately wanted). This company had already been through Techstars once and they had a year-and-a-half head start on us. So Techstars decided to reinvest in their own company by putting them through their accelerator again and gave them an incredible opportunity to work with the senior leaders at Disney (and get another round of investment).

So that's what brings us back to our acquaintance at One Million Cups. He was an investor in this company visiting Orlando and had heard of TROBO. The good news was that we were finally being noticed. That bad news was that we also got our first shot across the bow.

Emotions: Anger, determination.

Lesson(s) Learned: Don't let people get you down. Use those feelings to fire you up!

Preparing for Kickstarter

We'd planned from early on to be a Kickstarter company. That was our best way to raise capital and perform market validation without surrendering equity. Like many Kickstarters, we were naïve, thinking, "If you build it, they will come." Sometime in May, we began listening to Richard Bliss's "Funding the Dream", a weekly podcast on Kickstarter campaigns. After a few weeks, we began reading a blog by Jamey Stegmaier, and we read Tim Ferris's article. We started getting very scared. We realized there was a TON of work that needed to be done to make a Kickstarter successful. We learned you must build and bring your own crowd. We learned you must bring them on day 1 and 2, because there is a complex psychology around group mentality at play in Kickstarter. We learned that we should have a plan for marketing to someone somewhere every single day of the campaign. And we learned that social marketing involved giving something new to our networks that *they* could share to their networks. And we learned about the power of blogging, Google alerts, and social marketing tools.

Google Alerts
The basics of social marketing are that you need to give your network something of value to talk about. This is especially true when you are running a Kickstarter campaign, and you are posting something daily. We raised our antenna by signing up for keywords such as STEM, Engineering toys, etc. on Google Alerts. When we saw a topic of interest, we'd share that to our networks. That's a quick way to stay in touch with your industry and provide value to your followers.

Blogging
Another basic part of social marketing is to establish yourself as a learned expert in your given field. You listen, learn (ideally from the industry) form an opinion, and then share that opinion in the form of a blog or even a guest blog on someone else's blog. We learned this from Richard's show, and we reached out to Bess Auer, one of our good friends from the Starter Studio incubator. Bess runs Gotta Get Blogging, and is a significant influencer, because of her successful blog training courses and conventions. She taught us a bit about offering to other bloggers a list of things about which we could blog to add value to *their* audiences. She also kindly connected us with a few of her blogging friends, and we were able to blog for them and many others as guest bloggers during our campaign. We mainly discussed Engineering, STEM, and Management topics, because that is where we had street credibility. This kind of outreach leads to new followers who will ideally visit your site and sign up, or in our case, see the Kickstarter campaign and support us.

Social Marketing Works
We are GenX Engineers, so we were regular users of Facebook, Linked In, YouTube, and infrequent users of Twitter. And as for Pinterest – "umm, what is that?"

Being a user of a social network like Facebook and using them for marketing purposes are two different things. Facebook ads, Twitter ads, campaigns, etc.... are a large part of social marketing. We won't go into detail here, but we recommend that you do spend some time learning how these platforms work as marketing tools, when is the right time to run a campaign, how to use photos in the campaigns, etc.... For us, the basics were that we had a campaign every few days. We'd post something of value, a blog post, commentary on an article from Google alerts, other events in TROBO such as trade show updates and Kickstarter reach goals having been met, etc.... We didn't post "support our campaign" banners, which would have been cumbersome on day 10. We added value.

We learned about Hootsuite, an awesome tool that will allow you to schedule your tweets throughout the day. This was particularly helpful, when we were on a plane or driving or presenting somewhere, and we wanted a blog post to go out on our social media. We'd create the campaign art, upload a few versions to Hootsuite, and have them posted to our sites (Twitter, Facebook, LinkedIn, Google Plus, and apparently now you can do Instagram) at a preferred scheduled time, where we knew we'd get lots of looks. So for example, Monday morning at 10 am is a much better time slot to post than 10pm Sunday night. Some venues would get a single post, and some, like Twitter would get a variation on the post later in the day. We posted to Instagram and Pinterest separately, which took a bit more work. We always put in the time to include those sites, because our customers (Millenial Moms and Dads) were there. We took it to the people. Along the way we also heard about tools like If Then Than That, that were good at tracking feedback on events through social media. There were tools we never even got to try, but maybe next time we will learn more.

One of our biggest mistakes in preparing for our campaign was waiting too long to start marketing it. More accurately, we waited too long to start building our network for it. We hadn't befriended many bloggers by engaging them on their blogs months in advance. We hadn't befriended news reporters by reviewing and commenting on their articles months in advance or meeting them at events, etc.... *We learned late in our preparation efforts that news media were actually growing tired of Kickstarter stories.* More accurately, they were tired of the failures. If they reported on a Kickstarter, they wanted to report on a success. So if we didn't already know reporters, they really didn't want to be bombarded by yet another Kickstarter owner who was desperately trying to save his or her campaign. Apparently that had become pretty common, and the reporters (and even bloggers) felt used and overwhelmed with these types of requests. We were lucky in this respect, because we had become friends with many of our local tech community and reporters, and our own networks had some bloggers. Even our universities had some news outlets that helped spread the word in a timely fashion. But it would have been wise to participate in more bloggers' and news reporters' worlds as early as possible, getting to know them, and getting to know whether we could even add value.

Emotions: Surprise at how much work a Kickstarter is.

Lessons Learned: There are lots of social tools to help further your reach, and you need to start networking now for any Kickstarter you plan in the future. Warm calls to friends are much more successful than cold calls to strangers.

The Kickstarter Campaign

After months of building our campaign, and planning for our launch, our Kickstarter date was finally here. We couldn't really say we were completely ready; we still felt that we could do more to plan but sometimes you just have to take the leap. We had told our friends, family and network about the importance of supporting us on Day 1 of the campaign.

On September 3rd 2014, we crossed our fingers and clicked "Launch Campaign." We sent out messages on social media and via email to let people know that we had launched. The pledges started to come in quickly. By the end of the first day, we had raised over $18,000 from 120 backers. By getting almost 1/3 of the way towards our goal on the first day, we knew that our crowd had come!

On Day 2, things started out a little more quietly. After the incredible success of Day 1, we messaged out to people to thank them for their support and to encourage those who hadn't yet backed our campaign, to jump in on Day 2. We picked up another $3,000 on Day 2, which helped us cross the 33% level. We were incredibly excited.

Then, Day 3 rolled around. We looked at each other and said "Uh-oh." We had put so much emphasis on bringing our crowd to the table on Day 1, that we hadn't really thought of what to do on Day 3. We knew we would stay active on social media and try to "be someplace every day" but how could we drive supporters to back our campaign. We realized at that point that some backers might procrastinate and wait until the end to support us. The tough part was to stress the urgency of backing us without burning up all of our social currency with the people in our network and continuing to bug people. Easier said than done.

Kickstarter is a roller coaster. There is no other way to explain it. When you first start the process, you think, "This product is so cool, everyone will love it. It's definitely going to go viral!" Then, the more planning you do, the more you realize how difficult it is to cut through the clutter of all of the different products out there. How is my little project going to get any attention? So you plan and reach out to anyone and everyone who you think you can help. Then you cross your fingers and hope all of that work pays off.

For us, that first day was pure elation. We worked so hard to bring our crowd to Kickstarter and they definitely showed up. Days 2-30 were a mix of highs and lows. We learned that Richard Bliss was right - that no matter how long your Kickstarter campaign is, most campaign revenue charts look like the Golden Gate Bridge – high at the beginning, a trough in the middle and then (hopefully) another high at the end. The exceptions are those crazy viral successes like the Coolest Cooler that looks like a hockey stick – that keep on rising. So unless you go incredibly viral, you are going to have that low period in the middle – and your emotions will dip along with your revenues. The important part is to keep on moving; keep working throughout your campaign and keep your spirits up.

Emotions: Anxiety, fear.

Lesson(s) Learned: Plan ahead. Don't take a crowdfunding campaign lightly.

A Cease & Desist Letter – How You Know You Have Arrived
They say a small company knows they have finally arrived when they get their first cease and desist letter. Whether this is just a bucket list item for small companies, or is just an anecdote for entertainment purposes, TROBO did receive an infringement letter very early in the company's lifespan. It actually came via a next-day FedEx envelope the first week of our Kickstarter campaign. We had chosen the names of our TROBOs to honor engineers and innovators who we idolized. We weren't trying to capitalize on their names; it was simply a way to recognize people that we admired for their contributions to the world of STEM. We decided to name our male TROBO "Edison". Then, we got the letter from the Edison Foundation. In addition to various other efforts, the

Edison Foundation is in charge of overseeing the use of the Edison name. The letter we received told us that we must stop using the name Edison in all relationships associated with TROBO. As engineers we both hold Thomas Edison in the highest regard. He has impacted billions of people with his inventions. Our mistake was not knowing that we had to license his name.

Our second mistake was what got us into trouble. In our Kickstarter video we showed a photograph of Edison and we said that we named the character after Mr. Edison out of respect. By tying the name of our product together with a clear relationship to Mr. Edison, the Foundation said we needed to license the Edison name in order to do that. The letter was very courteous and actually mentioned that there may even be business opportunities where we could license Mr. Edison's name. We corresponded with the Foundation in hopes of doing just that, but unfortunately after further conversations we learned that they had already licensed the Edison name to another toy manufacturer who had exclusive rights for that product category.

This was sad news for us, because it meant changing the name of our first robot as well as changing all of the marketing materials for it. To make matters more interesting we were also in the middle of our Kickstarter campaign when all of this happened. This was a potential opportunity. We had a choice to make. We could be angry and try to play the "David versus Goliath" approach, which might have gotten us some free press. Or we could choose to change the name and handle it as best as we could. We chose the latter, for a couple of reasons. First the Edison Foundation representatives were courteous and professional, and they were just following through on their legal responsibility. The other reason was that our lawyer (and you should always have lawyers), advised us against picking a fight. Instead of making things harder, and potentially dragging our company and even our Kickstarter backers' money into some legal dispute down the line, we chose to change the name. We chose to make lemons out of lemonade.

We decided to have some fun by letting our Kickstarters get in on the action. We held a survey asking them for names that they thought would be great for TROBO. It was fun. We even illustrated a finish line with all of the top contenders for the names running beside each other. They were little TROBOs with word balloons above them with each name. In the end we had Newton as the winner with Nico and Tesla close behind. When we invent new TROBOs, we may revisit using those names since they were so popular. Within a month or so all of the references to Edison had been removed. We threw away marketing pamphlets, changed all of the website references, etc. and of course – within a few days of receiving the cease and desist letter – we removed the Edison reference from that video.

Emotions: stunned, dread, a sense of loss, then having fun with the turnaround

Lessons Learned: Namesakes are protectable. Do your homework if you get a cease and desist letter. People may just be doing their jobs in enforcing a protected property.

Maker Faire and the Science Museum

An important part of our Kickstarter strategy was being somewhere every single day during the campaign. For that reason, we planned our campaign around 2 major events – the ABC Kids Expo and Maker Faire Orlando.

The ABC Kids Expo in Las Vegas is one of the largest kids' products trade shows in America. We thought it would be a great opportunity to not only get feedback from retailers but also to get some attention from media and bloggers during our Kickstarter. We were excited to find out that the ABC Expo had a special Invention Connection showcase for startups to test out their products before they hit the market. It looked like a perfect fit and we were excited to be accepted into the showcase.

When we arrived at the show in Vegas, we discovered that while the Invention Connection was located on the exhibit floor, it was tucked into a corner and looked like an imposing fortress complete with walls and a guard at the front. While the showcase was open to companies that might want visitors to sign a Non-Disclosure Agreement prior to seeing their invention (and therefore wouldn't want just anyone roaming around), the reality was that all of the exhibitors were eager to get as much attention as they could. Unfortunately, the walls intimidated many potential visitors and booth traffic was low. All of the other innovators were incredibly friendly and supportive of each other so we all ended up encouraging anyone who came by to visit the other booths (some of us even walked them over to the next booth!) While we didn't get the exposure that we had hoped for, it was still a great experience and helped us to learn more about the industry and we made some great friends in the process.

Right after we returned from Las Vegas was Maker Faire Orlando. Maker Faire is a vast collection of people who build their own robots, gadgets, clothes, etc. We were offered a booth to show off TROBO and we happily accepted. It was a great opportunity to let adults and kids play with TROBO and we got tons of great feedback. It also allowed us to promote our Kickstarter campaign to a core audience (parents and kids who are excited about science and engineering). Over the weekend, we did over 600 demonstrations! We had almost no downtime over the two days (and we even brought in our wives to help with the crowds). It was a fantastic experience but it also made us realize something very important – over a week into our campaign, we realized that people still didn't know what Kickstarter (or crowdfunding) was. We had gone to great lengths to educate people about crowdfunding before the campaign but as we spoke to people at Maker Faire – people that knew about technology – many of them had never heard of Kickstarter. That was a problem.

Emotions: Exhilaration, exhaustion

Lessons Learned: Test, test, and then test some more. While you don't want to get into a situation where you are holding your product waiting for it to be perfect, you want to get your product in front of as many people as possible. Their feedback can be incredibly valuable, plus you never know how that one person can help you down the road.

"Wait, What is Kickstarter"?

Crowdfunding can be a tricky idea to understand. It's a relatively new concept and to ask people to give you money now so you can build a product later can be confusing. Before we launched our campaign, we made a video that explained the basics of crowdfunding. But as we went through our campaign, we continued to hear questions from potential backers: Is this a charity? (Nope. It's a real company.) Do I get stock in your company? (No, but you can pre-order your TROBO!) If you don't hit your goal, what happens to the money I paid? (Your credit card doesn't get charged unless we are successful). These basic questions made us realize our message wasn't getting through and forced us to concentrate our efforts on educating people about crowdfunding. We made follow-on videos and blogs on the subject, sending them out regularly to educate our crowd.

Emotions: Frustration, panic

Lessons Learned: Don't assume that your message has gotten through to everyone. Keep communicating and plan to educate your crowd.

Articles and news coverage

One of the ways we hoped to ride out the trough and – hopefully – see a spike in our Kickstarter pledges was through media. We reached out to every different media venue we could. In most cases, we were given the cold shoulder. In its early days, Kickstarter campaigns were stories in themselves. But now, as we mentioned, many media outlets were reluctant to report on a crowdfunding campaign until it already reached its goal and went viral (they didn't want to be seen as a free advertising campaign that would make a campaign successful). We were able to get some great local coverage from our local Fox affiliate as well as the Orlando Business Journal and Orlando Sentinel largely through our participation in Starter Studio (and because crowdfunding was still kind of new in Central Florida). But we couldn't break through to larger national media that would help us build our crowd.

We had a list of media outlets that we had created and we attempted to reach out to them with little success. One of the contacts on that list was from TechCrunch. TechCrunch is a very influential Silicon Valley news website that covers all aspects of technology. We had heard of the "TechCrunch Effect"; crowdfunding campaigns that were featured in TechCrunch often saw an immediate boost that dramatically altered their campaign revenue curve. Through a contact, we reached out to the reporter at TechCrunch and told her our story. She agreed to write a story but we had no idea when it would be published and if it would be in time to save our Kickstarter. We believe the reason we got her attention, was because we were presenting at an event she normally attended, which gave us some credibility.

On iPhone 6 launch day, Jeremy was at the local Apple store when his phone buzzed and a message said that TROBO had a new Kickstarter backer. At the time, we were getting between 2 and 4 backers a day. All of the sudden, another message popped up and then another. Then a Twitter notification popped up that mentioned TROBO and TechCrunch. Jeremy sat down at a computer in the Apple store and launched TechCrunch. The headline on TechCrunch on iPhone 6 launch day was not the lines at Apple stores around the world but instead, it was a storytelling plush robot! Maybe this would get us the bump that we needed? Jeremy went around the store launching the TechCrunch story on as many computers as possible and left the store. Our Twitter feed blew up and – all of the sudden – we were getting lots of attention. It felt great to have new people – far from our traditional network – noticing TROBO and backing our campaign. And it happened right in the middle of the campaign.

Emotions: Elation.

Lessons Learned: Keep networking to get attention to your product/company. You never know what you can get, if you just kindly ask.

Power of PR, but a bit late

Despite our ability to get some buzz, we were still a ways off from hitting our Kickstarter goal and time was running short. We decided to hire a PR company in the last two weeks of the campaign to help drive additional media coverage. We reached out to a company who we had met at the ABC Kids Expo that specialized in mommy product PR. They provided us with a tenacious account manager who used her skills to reach out to contacts at major media outlets around the country. While we had some great opportunities, we weren't able to capitalize on all of them as many wanted samples and – at the time – we only had 4 TROBOs and since the app wasn't yet in the App Store, we would have to send them an iPad too. For a small company with limited resources, this was a risky proposition. In fact, when we tried to reach out to a blogger on our own and we sent her a TROBO and an iPad, she didn't send it back for months. Needless to say, with one of our 4 prototypes out of our hands we were very nervous. We were able to get some great coverage from bloggers through the efforts of the PR company but we always regretted the morning shows and other opportunities that slipped away.

Emotions: Regret that we didn't tap this resource earlier.

Lessons learned: Plan your PR as a timely part of your campaign, not as a hail mary.

The Final Weekend: Going Back to the Well

We both felt that we had spent most of our "social currency" with the campaign with the constant messaging to our social networks and asks for support. We jokingly said we'd never get a job in Orlando again. But from one of the blogs or podcasts we listened to late in the campaign, we learned that actually people probably weren't bothered and would want to help, if they could. So that final Saturday, we went back to the well, and we learned one of the biggest lessons a Kickstarter should understand. Explain to your backers in the final day or two that if they just upgrade their order by "this tiny amount" from one tier to the next, in aggregate, they would push the campaign over the top. We made an easy-to-understand infographic showing that impact. The results were mind-blowing, and we leapt another $10K towards our goal.

Emotions: surprise, humility, and excitement

Lessons Learned: Go back to the well at the end, and show your current backers how their small contribution can help in a big way.

The Final Minutes of Our Campaign
On October 8th we had been watching our computers and phones nonstop as we tried to remind people of the critical nature of our Kickstarter coming to an end. We had planned and executed on updates to all of our social media every hour then every half hour then every 15 minutes and finally almost by the minute as we were trying to bring in our $60,000 before we lost it all. What we didn't know at that point was how many other people were also watching the clock with us. In the months following the end of our Kickstarter we would hear from friends and family that they all were watching to see whether we would make our $60,000 goal. We met complete strangers who told us they were also watching until the last minute to see whether we would actually pull this thing together. It was humbling to know how many of our friends cared enough to root for us, and some even significantly increased their bids at the last minute so that we could make our dream into a reality.

When we initially set our Kickstarter goal, we knew we really needed around $100,000, but we also knew that $100,000 would also feel insurmountable to anyone contributing $60 or some investment amount to make it a reality. We were not celebrities with thousands of followers, but we did have decent networks that we brought to the table. And we had spent almost all of our social currency bringing those networks to our campaign.

…

11:42 PM

11:43 PM

…

In our giddy state Jeremy - being a bit desperate for creativity - decided to offer a joke for every pledge that was made. It actually seemed to work, and so bad science joke after bad science joke, Jeremy helped to pull us closer to our $60,000 goal. Near the end of this, Chris began to worry that our backers would believe we were being disingenuous or that we had it made and therefore would pull their pledges. So to Jeremy's chagrin Chris asked him to stop and he did.

At midnight we found ourselves staring at a $61,000 successful Kickstarter. We were excited for about 10 minutes, and then the reality set in - we would have to execute and deliver on our promise. What a day. What an evening. What an hour. We both knew at that point that $60,000 would only get us the absolute bare bones version of TROBO, but it was enough to start. We knew that, if necessary, we would have to put more money in, but the plan, if we could not find further sales or funding, was for Chris to do all of the illustration and development work and deliver a very basic, non-scalable version of the application.

Fortunately, that was not the route we had to take. God, Fate, Friends, and Family are helping us make this journey, and good things had only begun.

Emotions: Stress, elation, relief, fatigue

Lessons Learned: Never underestimate the power of your friends, family, and even strangers, to come through for you at the last minute.

After Kickstarter – Putting the Pieces in Place

Now that we finished our campaign, it was time to get our ducks in a row and deliver on our campaign. The learning process continued.

Patents
The patent process was somewhat new for us. We had both been a part of patenting discussions before, but we had not created one for our own products. Working in our co-working space and building our network with Starter Studio, we had met a few IP lawyers along the way. In fact it seems that IP lawyers regularly network with startups, because of course that is where IP is often created. Entrepreneurs start a company and almost invariably get asked, "Do you have a patent?" We had spoken with a few IP lawyers, but we chose one that we were friends with in Canvs, and who had also supported us on Kickstarter. Shanti was a Biology major who became a lawyer, so the opportunity to combine those skills to gave her a unique technically savvy position in the industry.

We bonded very well, and she began to write the patents with us and guided us on what to do. Before starting, we knew we needed legal expertise, but we both felt that – if needed – we could have written the patent on our own. That was *not* true. We learned that there is so much legal jargon in a patent to make it strong and enforceable that we would have clearly been out of our league. We spent a significant amount of time in November creating the provisional patent. (A provisional patent is like a placeholder; it lets you hold your place in line as you claim an invention. By itself, it is not a patent application; you still need to file a non-provisional patent.) The provisional patent did not need to have many of the required claims that the non-provisional patent would need. However we spent a significant time writing the provisional patent as closely as we could get it to the non-provisional patent.

All of the drawings were completed and most of the claims were in place.

Shanti was very proficient at guiding us through the process but also understanding our product. The hardware in the product is fairly technical, and the usage scenarios are also reasonably complicated at least with respect to how it must be patented. But that was no problem for her. She knew what she was doing and helped us to clarify the holes in our application and position us for strength. Later in March we submitted the non-provisional patent which had effectively the same things as the provisional with some extra clarifications and detail. As of the writing of this book we are still in the dark period, where we are waiting for the application to be processed.

Like many companies, if TROBO is unsuccessful it will probably fail in the market long before we ever learn whether or not the patent was awarded by the US Patent and Trademark Office. But we were excited to have the protection that even this level of coverage gives us, and we would recommend it to anyone who believes they will eventually search for funding. What we have found is that most investors won't be interested in investing in you if you do not have patent protection. Often times the patent is not the biggest factor in whether you are successful. It is your ability to access the market and sell that determines your success or failure. The only way a patent is useful is if you have the money to fight for what you were trying to protect. If a large company eats your breakfast they probably have deeper pockets anyway and can keep you in court until you drain all of your funds trying to fight for your IP. However, nonetheless without a patent everyone tends to see your technology as unprotected and therefore un-investable. As it is, not only do we have a patent in process, but we also have a clear vision for the next-generation of TROBO and the generations after that. There is something to be said for considering where your product or your company will be in five years. Developing a patent on your current technology will also force you to think about your future technologies.

Emotions: Overwhelmed.

Lessons Learned: Patents are a reasonable amount of work, can be expensive, and can distract you from your core service or R&D. Be sure you are getting decent protection and value for it before starting the process. For some companies/products, they may not be necessary. If you are going to be looking for outside investment, they are an essential part of the conversation.

Hiring a Development Team

Hiring a development team has a myriad of aspects that must be considered. Acting as a Technical Director of your product, you need to determine all of the things that you are going to deal with in the coming years. In our scenario being a startup with limited funds we could not hire developers and artists directly under a salaried position. That's a larger commitment that would take more budget then we would have for a while. So we knew we were going to just be dealing with contract labor. Contractors come in a variety of forms and it is often difficult to find people that you can work with and trust. Chris had years of experience working with contractors so he reached out to his network and found companies he had worked with before and who he trusted. Jeremy and Chris had also met one of the contract companies while networking for TROBO. So we created a request for quote or RFQ. The RFQ was a high-level feature list. Not only did it have business features, but it also had technical requirements of the technology and technology stacks we were considering, functional diagrams, and of course the technical skills necessary to deliver. The next step was to send the RFQ out to the teams and hope that the budgets they sent back were not significantly different than our internal estimates used for Kickstarter.

Of course you should have the skills necessary to at least have a reasonable idea of what the numbers will look like when they come back. If you don't this is a good sign that you have a problem with your management team. We have seen several companies whose core IP is something that they don't understand. If you're developing something highly technical, and you don't have a highly technical person who is an expert in that area on your team, stop right now and find that person. It is critical that you have someone on your team to understand your IP at least enough to guide other companies and who understands how to keep control of the IP when you are using contractors. If you want to go on a learning effort and learn the technology yourself, that's great too. You can do that. Just understand you are signing yourself up to do so. If you hire a company to develop your IP, and they control it, you will be in very big trouble in just a few of years.

So we sent our RFQ to 3 to 4 companies. We knew going into it that the companies would recommend technologies that they were familiar with, because of their experience working with it. Unfortunately, while this allowed us to explore using four different technologies, it made the technical decision harder, because not only were we gauging the communications and technical skills of the companies, we were also gauging the power of the platforms and technologies they were recommending. We had the potential to work in several platforms since this was a mobile application. We looked at Flash, PhoneGap, Titanium, Unity, Cocos 2-D, native C, and Objective-C, because all of these were going to run on the iPhone first. Later we intended to go to Android, so we wanted the ability to support multiple platforms.

So when we reviewed the quotes, we not only assessed their proposed budgets but we also looked at the technology architecture they were proposing as well as their skills in those architectures. This is a really big decision for any company because it will affect the entire future of the company and your company could fail if you make the wrong decision here. By the first week in December we had reviewed all of the quotes and chosen our partner company. They happened to be very good friends of Chris's from his previous work experience. It was difficult not to choose some of the other companies, especially those with whom we had a personal relationship. The other companies that provided quotes also did a solid job but the combination of technology skills, speed, other commitments that they would have and even dynamics around having two companies work together led to Jeremy and Chris picking RealVisualz out of Seattle and Kosovo. RealVisualz was run by two guys named Ridvan and Steven and they had other partners that have come in along the way. They have an education platform called EDUOnGo which is a portal for creating your own class online. That was also a plus because Chris and Jeremy knew that if they were successful in their NSF SBIR grant application, they would be investigating an education platform with a portal for schools.   So the partnership made even more sense than perhaps working with some of the other companies, because we knew we might build TROBO EDU on top of EDUOnGo's platform. And that is actually what we did. So the decision to choose the team worked out very well and they are still working with us today.

Emotions: Pleased we had the money to execute on TROBO with a team.

Lessons Learned: Pick your team based on talent and current skillsets, if you don't have the budget to train them up on your preferred platform. Also, trust is more important than price. Finally, make sure that you ask for more money than you need to complete your product. There are many Kickstarter campaigns that succeeded in hitting their goal but failed to deliver because they didn't raise enough to deliver.

An old friend at LaserPegs and Another Mentor

About 6 months into TROBO, Chris got a call from Rob, an old friend from his early days in the comic book industry. Rob had gone from being a comic book Illustrator and Inker to a Senior VP at Laser Pegs, a light-up brick building game manufacturer in Sarasota, Florida. He was just calling to catch-up, and as the conversation went on, they recognized there was a mentoring opportunity there. Soon we drove over, and met with Rob and Laser Pegs' Founder, Jon Capriola. Jon was a serial entrepreneur, and together he and Rob began providing powerful insights, not only into retail packaging as mentioned in the packaging section, but also into the big, scary world of retail toy sales.

Jon gave us some stories of tough love and sacrifice as he built his very successful enterprise. He had created several other startup concepts before striking success. The advice he gave, and still continues to give, is always real and honest. His company was many years ahead of ours, so he was able to tell us his choices in similar situations and the ramifications of those choices. Rob also had insights into packaging design, sales, dealing with toy reps, and dealing with manufacturers.

Emotions: Joy at finding a mentor in an old friend and a new friend that were geographically so close.

Lessons Learned: You never know where mentorship can come from. People like to mentor; just ask questions but respect their time.

Packaging Design

Designing the TROBO packaging provided its own challenges. Chris had two years of Industrial Design training before switching to Engineering at Auburn, and he had done packaging design as a student. We knew roughly the kind of package we would need to be on the toy shelf. We worked on a couple of different designs; we went to the local toy stores and photographed a bunch of items that were comparable. We created a variety of early sketches.

Through surveys and packaging reviews, the color scheme, the logo, and the package were annealed into one cohesive brand identity. The website of course was also updated to reflect the new myTROBO brand. The box started out as an open faced design, with bright orange, bright yellow, bright green, and we prototyped the box from large sheets of cardboard, and large sheets of matte board because the thickness was right, and the rigidity was enough to represent the final product. We also made scale models at one-quarter scale to quickly iterate. During this period, we started working with our friends at Laser Pegs, who provided instruction and good feedback on what made a product have nice sell-through on a retail shelf. Chris could tell Rob really had a passion and understanding of what was important for a package on the shelf.

With all of the feedback we were getting, we felt good about the packaging. The following May, however, we did put in a "Try Me" feature where the child could reach in and touch the TROBO's hand. We had been telling everyone how cuddly the toys were but the acetate window we added kept them from feeling it.

By the end of January, we had made a significant change in the box. Most of the physical layout had been built, but the color scheme was just not working. It said. "I am a $25 product." We needed to tell the public that this was a $60 product. So we had a brand problem where the packaging was geared towards children and towards the toy aisle, instead of a high-tech connected toy buyer in the tech aisle. At some point while we were talking with a manufacturer's rep that was very savvy with tech toys like ours, they explained the retail impact of being in two converging markets - technology and toys. They explained that other companies were doing this as well, but finding themselves on the tech shelves and not on the traditional toy shelves. While the toy shelves may sound appealing, they also were much more competitive and typically had a much lower margin than the electronics/connected toy shelves. This was a wake up call, because it meant we had to differentiate ourselves away from the lower-end toy aisle and towards the appropriately higher-end tech aisle. We *wanted* to be on that aisle, both for brand purposes and for a better margin opportunity.

We looked at Apple and Best Buy stores and we saw the pristine white boxes of the traditional Apple devices and toys that were positioning themselves as connected toys intended to be in Apple stores. They communicated the high-end experience we were creating with TROBO. So that's what we did. For some designs the box was overly complicated with too much information and, with others, the box was extremely simple. To achieve the austere look that Apple had on their boxes, we removed almost all of the artwork and started from scratch. We started with only a white box and added colors to the logo as needed. We also chose foil, which would communicate a premium product.

Foil does add to the expense of the packaging but the value that it brings is worth the price. When people look at our boxes, they no longer think this is a $25 toy on a Wal-Mart shelf. They see it as a more expensive connected experience that you would find at an Apple store. The white also works for the TROBO brand, because white clean pastel colors are often used to communicate youthful brands.

The initial boxes for TROBO list the Kickstarter supporters who supported us through our campaign before the halfway point. This was a promotional effort by us to get backers in as early as possible. Now the boxes are collector's items, because only 2000 of them have ever been made with a backers list and a reference to Kickstarter. The same is also true for the toys. So when TROBOs are shipping by the thousands, as we certainly hope they will, those Kickstarter backers and early buyers this past year really do have something special that no other buyers will be able to get. Once the first run is done, we are removing the Kickstarter backer list from the packaging and from the sewing label on the back of the TROBO. This will be exciting for us, because it will mean that we made it past Kickstarter and are starting to become a real company. The future packaging design for TROBO could change of course we have ideas for TROBO 2.0 and 3.0 and we also have ideas around the TROBO backstory. Just as we are able to do more storytelling with TROBOs, the packaging and brand will evolve with them.

Emotions: Fun. Packaging design is a bit of a guilty pleasure.

Lessons Learned: You can pivot in every aspect of your business, even packaging design. You can have mentors in new industries. Ask lots of questions, and learn everything you can. You should pay it forward, just like they did for you.

Year 2: Building a Company, Not Just a Product

While we were focusing on execution, we were also continuing to keep our eyes open for bigger opportunities to build the company and really launch the TROBO brand.

Kevin Hale and Applying to Y-Combinator

Y-Combinator (Y-C) was one of the highest profile business incubators in the world. Companies from all over longed to be a part of the program in order to be catapulted into the big time. We were focused on executing on TROBO when we met one of the partners at Y-C.

We met Kevin Hale a couple months before, when he was visiting Orlando. We got some great advice from him about getting the unit out even sooner than we had planned. He invited us to apply, so we did, late of course, because that's apparently how we roll. In addition to our application to Y-C, we also purchased a safety vest for Kevin Hale. The safety vest was this ugly bright orange and neon green color that you might use as a crossing guard or some other safety person. You may be saying "That seems like an odd choice" but we had done our homework. We read online on his Twitter feed that he was really into vests. So we bought him the most garish vest we could find on Amazon and had it sent to the Y-C office along with a note. The note said, "Kevin we got you this safety vest, because TROBO is about to blow your mind." We hoped of course that it would help us stand out just a little bit from the crowd. We never heard back from Kevin whether or not our vest made it to him, but we have to think that it caught someone's eye at Y-C and maybe helped our application get through the door based on creativity.

Our late application caused us to be in a last minute batch of interviewees just before Christmas. We weren't going to pass up the golden opportunity however, so we hopped the plane and took off to Silicon Valley. While we were in town, we continued our standard "Where's TROBO?" photo bombs, snapping up shots of Newton and Curie at Apple, Google, Y-C, and IDEO.

The Y-C experience was a mix of surprise, competition, intensity, and humility. We arrived at a very unassuming Y-C building, which looked like a one floor, set of offices surrounding a common meeting area. No frills. This place was austere, on purpose. We waited in the common area and enjoyed meeting a few of the other approximately 20 companies waiting their turn in the hot seat. We all focused on the myriad questions we had read that they ask, and we practiced answering our most common rejections. Every product has problems or concerns or even just general questions. As entrepreneurs or salespeople doing over a thousand demos, we knew the common questions. What we were most concerned with, was what we didn't know. It was our first live investor pitch.

Our time came up. We sat down and looked at the four interviewers. They courteously let us give our one-minute pitch. They began asking questions, and it was immediately clear that they could not see the way to scale TROBO into a multibillion-dollar business. We have heard a few times that the real stars in the Y-Combinator program are Software As A Service (SAAS) companies that could scale into the billions.

We definitely felt we had a multimillion-dollar business, but it required a lot of capital to get us there. One of our interviewers had a background in education technology. Overall the conversation went fine, and we answered questions, but the education investor was aggressive in his questioning. Five minutes goes by very quickly when you're being grilled on your company, and there's always something you forget. We forgot to mention our grant in that interview, and we believe that hurt our ability to get into the program. When you are projecting only several million dollars in sales, a program like Y-C becomes less interested.

We received the prompt reply via email that we did not make it into the program. Their main reason was that they did not believe we would be ready by the end of the incubation period. They were correct. We were not planning to ship units by the end of the program, but it sort of felt like a courteous "thanks, but no thanks". Considering they were interviewing several hundred companies that day, and several thousand for the opportunity, we understood they couldn't be too detailed in their reply.

Our preparation for Y-C was to use a mobile app that a friend of ours had given us with all the Y-C questions he could find on the Internet. All the questions asked by Y-C have been documented for the most part somewhere. We added our answers, and it became a flash card experience on our phones. It was tremendously helpful, because it allowed us to read the questions while were waiting, sitting on the airplane etc. We drilled each other on the questions, playing investor and investee. Even though we did not get into Y-C, we felt honored that they showed interest in the project. To us it meant further validation that there was opportunity out there, and that people saw the opportunity in this emerging market (and in TROBO). They were correct. We would not have been ready to ship TROBO by the end of the program, however we already knew that. Even though we missed out on that opportunity, we are now stronger than ever, and we have a product that has been truly annealed to be a solid experience for children and parents.

Emotions: Excitement, apprehension, and melancholy.

Lessons Learned: Your startup is often about the journey and not just about the end goal. Enjoy it.

Networking: Anki
While we were in the Bay Area for our Y-C interview, everyone suggested, that we use the opportunity (and the free trip) to meet with someone. The problem was, who would we meet? We didn't have any connections to Venture Capitalists, and we had less than a week's notice. Jeremy was scheduled to be a panelist at the Digital Kids Expo and noticed that one of the other companies – Anki – had a Penn alum named Mark as a co-founder. Jeremy reached out to him the day before we were to travel to California, and Mark was kind enough to rearrange his schedule to meet with us. Although relatively new to the toy industry, Anki had raised hundreds of millions of dollars and had an incredibly successful product called Anki Drive. Mark was able to give us a primer on

their entry to the industry, lessons learned and refer us to some of the people that helped them get their product placed in major retailers. He also explained that they considered themselves a platform company first, and a toy company second. This rang true to how we saw TROBO, and this perspective would later find itself surfacing in our proforma projections for the Phase 2 SBIR grant and in our investor pitch. It was another example of how you never know who you might meet and how people are willing to help each other, if you just ask.

Emotions: Gratitude at their kindness and willingness to share

Lessons Learned: If you are fortunate enough to make a business trip to make a pitch, make the most of it. Network and see if there is anyone else you can meet while you are visiting.

Getting the Phase 1 NSF Grant
The week before our Y-C visit, the National Science Foundation awarded us a Phase 1 SBIR grant. So the emotional roller coaster ride continued.

The NSF grant started paying in January, and it worked wonders for our ability to create a better quality app while allowing us to focus on the business too. We were able to hire artists from the Florida Interactive Entertainment Academy in Orlando that was founded by the city, UCF, and EA SPORTS.

Under the grant, the team grew to have 4 Artists and one Developer in addition to the Engineering team out of Kosovo. While Chris was driving content production and engineering, Jeremy was driving the research around creating TROBO EDU. The NSF grant was given to us as a Phase 1 opportunity to explore whether TROBOs could be used in schools.

Specifically we were investigating whether TROBOs could create value in kindergarten and prekindergarten environments. Jeremy began doing interview after interview after interview with teachers, principals, administrators, and educational institutions. In true entrepreneurial fashion we followed a lean startup methodology, which is required by the NSF to do the validation of the business concept. Jeremy interviewed over 50 teachers to gather information, and then he and Chris designed additional features, including a journal application and the beginnings of what would become TROBO EDU. Teachers wanted to have a backend server to which they could upload the content. They wanted to have journals to track what the children were learning, and they wanted more from the toy.

We learned that some schools did not know what to do with the TROBO toy. This is one of those examples where when you're creating a new product and pushing a new kind of market, people don't quite know what to do with your technology. This is where as the one inventing the product or creating market, you have to figure that out with your customer. So Jeremy did several rounds of interviews, and Chris would do the product iterations. At the end of the grant the TROBO application had several improvements including better content at a higher quality experience that really felt like AA, if not AAA, quality.

The company had also built the prototype of the TROBO Diary journal app and a prototype of the educational portal. We also built some next-generation prototypes for what we eventually called TROBO 2.0 and put some of those items in front of teachers for initial feedback. Some of the responses were stronger than others on the given features, and of course those responses guided our decisions about the next-generation hardware development.

The grant gave us the opportunity to do a deep dive into the education market. As we spoke to more teachers and administrators, it became obvious that many early childhood teachers felt uncomfortable teaching STEM because of their own backgrounds; they may have only had one or two science classes in their own teacher training. We recognized that we could solve this problem with teacher guides and supplementary information that teachers could use with their TROBO stories to feel comfortable introducing STEM to their classroom. We worked with teachers and experts at the University of Central Florida to prototype these resources and we put them in front of teachers to get their feedback. The result was a comprehensive curriculum format for using TROBO to teach STEM to young children. We had proven feasibility.

By the end of May, the team was up to 12 part time employees. They could move very quickly. Jeremy ran the operations and Chris ran the product development.

Emotions: Elation at getting the grant and seeing it transform the company.

Lessons Learned: Grants can be a huge help for entrepreneurs. Search for grants that can help you. It's very hard to apply, but it can open doors and provide further validation that you are solving a problem people care about.

Choosing a Domain Name and social handle... twice

One mistake we made in our Startup Weekend rush was picking a long social handle. We chose our tagline as "Here comes TROBO", a delightful play on "Here comes Trouble". That was fun, and we still use that phrase in some marketing today. We also picked herecomestrobo.com. About 10-15 years ago, if you grabbed your domain of choice, you were gold. If not, you would get a different dot COM and choose a new company name. We eventually grabbed the herecomestrobo social handles, and we used those throughout our Kickstarter campaign. It was late in the campaign that we began to realize just how expensive each letter in a social handle can be, especially when the bulk of your social marketing goes through Twitter. When people retweet your tweets they need space in the 140-character limit. And when people refer to you as "I'm excited to get @herecomestrobo today", your brand moans a bit, as a phrase doesn't work well as a noun.

So in January of 2016, after also writing thousands of emails with a really long domain name, we went back to the drawing board to see how close to *just* using TROBO as our social as we could get. We used a wonderful website called Knowem.com that will let you search for your favorite handle and domain across 80+ sites. They'll even set up all the accounts for you for a reasonable fee.

Even though (we thought) TROBO was a made-up word, we couldn't get the "TROBO" social handles. We considered iTROBO, and pluralizing the brand to TROBOs and TROBOes. Based on internal discussions about brand, new logo sketches, and on what we could actually find, we chose myTROBO. That solved our Twitter problems by reducing our tweet footprint from 14 characters to 7, and it made people referring to us feel more natural: "I'm excited to get @myTROBO today". It also is much less cumbersome to write emails with the smaller domain, so our corporate feng shui is improved. At the same time we reduced our brand's color scheme from 16 to 3.

Even after nearly 9 months of transitioning to the new social handle, we still have active herecomestrobo email accounts and old marketing materials. We expect it will stick around for another 1-2 years before we finally have cleared all the connections to that domain. In the meantime we have domain forwards, old twitter and Facebook accounts, etc....

Emotions: Annoyance.

Lessons Learned: Stop. Research. And put some serious thought into your social handle before you start sharing it with the world. It's worth the extra stitch in time to save 9... characters.

Lessons Relearned: Put more thought into your design choices; SIMPLIFY. Think about what it will take to produce all of the marketing collateral that you may need (brochures, business cards, t-shirts, etc.). Are your logo choices going to cost you more money in the long run?

Our 2nd Trip to Toy Fair
In February of 2015, TROBO made its first appearance at the New York International Toy Fair. While Jeremy had walked the show the year before, TROBO was featured on the show floor in the

Launchpad pavilion for startups. We had a small, tabletop display that enabled us to display TROBO and to try to sell. The only problem is that we weren't sure when we would have TROBOs to sell, so we weren't aggressively courting big retailers. Also, because we knew that the largest retailers have complicated merchandising and logistics procedures that are difficult for a small company like ours to tackle, we knew we wanted to start with direct sales and smaller retailers first before approaching the "big box" retailers. Despite being told by one of our mentors to expect little-to-no sales at Toy Fair, we felt like we missed out by not leaving with a big stack of orders.

Pitching Three Toy Manufacturers
At Toy Fair, we had the opportunity to meet with 3 major toy manufacturers. We would love to tell you their names, but we had to sign a Non-Disclosure Agreement (NDA) and we would love to not get sued. A Non-Disclosure Agreement is a legal document between two parties that says what you can (and what you can't) talk about. It is very common in business to be presented with an NDA to sign and many companies won't even start to have a discussion with you without signing one. Think carefully before you sign anything and decide whether it's worth it to you.

During the show, high-level representatives from the companies came by the booth to check out TROBO. They watched our demonstration and gave us feedback. It was nerve-wracking. These people could either make or break us. One company ended up sending 10 people to the booth over the course of the show. We felt like this meant that either they were interested in pursuing a relationship, or they wanted to rip us off. The reality is, if a major manufacturer wanted to copy our product, all of the intellectual property protection in the world – patents, trademarks, etc. – wouldn't mean a thing if you don't have the money to defend your property. But – supposedly – there is an unwritten code in the industry; since many of the newest toys on the market are often created by other companies or consultants and then either sold or licensed to the big toy manufacturers, if word got around that they were stealing people's ideas, no one would show them anything anymore. Once again, being new to the industry, we had to put some faith in that unwritten rule.

Our expectations during these meetings were tempered. We weren't expecting one of the companies to present us with a giant, Publishers Clearing House-style check to license (or buy) our idea. But we were hoping for a follow-up meeting. We didn't hear back from two of the companies but thankfully, the third company (the one that sent all of the people to our booth), agreed to meet with us at their corporate offices.

Emotions: Disappointment from a sense of lack-luster sales performance at the tradeshow. Elation at the huge potential from landing a follow-up licensing meeting.

*Lessons Learned: Manage your expectations when you attend a tradeshow. Before you go, make a list of the top people you would want to meet and focus on getting those people to your booth. It's not about who can collect the most business cards; it's about meeting the **right** people.*

"You Haven't Been Selling? What?"

When you are starting a business – especially a product business, selling is everything. Unfortunately, selling was a problem for us. We certainly believed in our product and our mission but we were trying to jump into an unfamiliar market and we were still learning. We continued to learn about the big box sales cycle – choosing their holiday product mix a year ahead of time. But we also consciously made a choice that the big box stores couldn't be our first channel. Jeremy knew from one of his college friends who was a VP at a major retail chain about the perils of retail merchandising requirements; some stores have a 200 page document specifying all of their rules for how product needs to arrive at their stores and warehouses – UPC codes need to be located exactly here, your product needs to be labeled with these specific items, etc. Failure to abide by every single rule can result in chargebacks – stores will deduct money from what they owe you to cover any "handling" of your product by their employees. Miss enough rules and you could end up having to write a check to the store instead of getting paid by them. For a small company trying to ship their first units, that prospect was daunting. Plus, the quantities that they were talking about seemed beyond our reach – how could we afford to build 100,000 units? Therefore, we decided to focus on selling directly through our website, some online channels and smaller boutique retailers.

But our experience at Toy Fair showed us that we still had a lot to learn. People said they loved the product but – aside from the continuous flow of pre-orders on our website and great press – we weren't getting interest from retailers. We figured that our profile – being at trade shows, media mentions, some ongoing social media – would be enough to have orders coming in but it wasn't. The reality was that we weren't focused on selling. Between development of the app and stories, our NSF grant and just keeping manufacturing moving, we weren't making the phone calls.

This is where being primarily a two-person company really hurt us. We knew we were missing that "third leg of the stool", an experienced salesperson who could take the product and run with it. But as we talked about it, we also realized there were limits. We had questions. "How do we compensate such a person without investment capital? How do we align our expectations with theirs? It would be great if they could go out tomorrow and sell a million units, but we don't even have units to ship yet. What would we do, if they brought in a 10K unit order?" These are all problems that small product companies face, but unfortunately, we didn't have the answers. We began talking with mentors in the toy space, toy reps, manufacturers reps, and we began the steep learning curve of retail toy sales. By the summer we were making follow-up phone calls to boutique retailers, museum store retailers, and direct sales retailers trying to close small volume sales before their fall budgets had all been spent. At the time of this book's writing, we are still learning, and still know we have plenty to learn. We are also still building relationships with sales reps.

Emotions: A sense of failure and surprise when finally recognizing our biggest weakness

Lessons Learned: Make sure you have a balanced team from the beginning – development, manufacturing, sales and marketing (and find experienced mentors that can help fill the gaps)... or prepare to embark on yet another learning curve.

Attempting to license our platform

When we first learned about licensing our product to another company, everything about it seemed wrong. While it can take many forms, licensing can often mean that someone else takes care of the manufacturing, marketing and distribution of the product. They take the lion's share of the revenue in return for taking the risk, and you get a royalty for creating the concept. When you are initially looking at making $15-$20 per unit in profit, a royalty of $1 per unit seems pretty lousy.

Until, that is, you factor in all of the costs involved in getting those units to market – financing your inventory, paying for shelf space, logistics, marketing, advertising, etc. All of that gets very expensive, very quickly. For us, the more we learned about the toy industry, the harder it seemed it would be to get TROBO into peoples' hands. All of the sudden, licensing seemed like a good option for us. Except there was one additional complication – TROBO is not a static product that gets developed once and sold. The heart of the TROBO concept was our continuous development of new content for our tablet app. That means that unlike someone who builds a board game, licenses it and collects their royalty, we needed to continuously invest in content development in order to get recurring revenue. So any potential licensing partner would need to invest in development as well (and split our story revenue with us).

We flew to the corporate offices of the company we met at Toy Fair. We asked them in advance what questions and concerns they had about TROBO. We prepared for every possible question they would ask and we had to decide how much we would share about our vision for the future of TROBO. We also researched our core customer – millennial moms who wanted to give their kids a head start in education and were also more than likely reasonably comfortable with "tablet time."

There was a good showing from their side with many of their top executives and designers. We went through our presentation and tried to sound confident. They asked many of the questions we had prepared for, and they were even kind enough to share some of their insights about their decades of experience in early childhood product design. We left behind some TROBOs for them to play with, and we scheduled a follow-up call to figure out how we could move forward together. Walking out, we felt that we had blown a potential opportunity. Instead of having a discussion, that involved everyone in the room and brought them into the process, we had done a presentation. It may not have made a difference in the long run but it seems like we had approached our meeting with the wrong strategy.

A few weeks later, we had our follow-up call. They decided to pass, explaining that they liked the overall concept but already had some similar products in development. They were very transparent about their thoughts and opinions on what we were trying to do with TROBO and we were grateful for their insights. We thanked them and decided to move forward on our own. Later, we were disappointed to find out that they were already working with one of our competitors on a new product for the holidays. Once again, it showed us how much we still had to learn.

Emotions: Disappointment and frustration with our own inability to turn an opportunity into a sale. Gratitude that a company of such magnitude would give us the time to pitch them TROBO.

Lessons Learned: Sell; don't present. When you have a big customer presentation, make sure you know what you want to get out of it. Don't be afraid to ask questions to tailor the discussion to their needs. Listen to Zig Zigler's sales training to learn how to "Lead with Need". We were listening to this, but we did not execute it well for that pitch. Hard lessons learned.

Sales Reps and TV Shows Selling *Us*

So we knew we had a sales problem and we knew we needed some help. We started to learn about the role of manufacturers' representatives in the toy industry. Manufacturers' reps handle multiple manufacturers and they leverage their relationships with retail channels to create a sort of phantom sales force for toy companies. The idea is that since it would be costly for companies to build and sustain an outside sales team with those relationships, why not outsource sales to someone who specializes in it. In return, they are compensated based on their sales; if they don't sell, you don't pay. Sounds like a no-lose proposition, right? However, there are a few complications. The first is that your product can easily get lost in their product portfolio. If they carry too many brands, they will focus on the ones that are most lucrative for them; if that is not your brand, then you can quickly become an afterthought. Second, you need to make sure your product is aligned with their portfolio. Many of the reps that initially contacted us carried baby and kid products – strollers, car seats, pacifiers, etc. – instead of toys. And the reality was that we weren't even sure that a straight-up toy rep would be perfect for us since we straddled the line between toys and consumer electronics (the new "Connected Toy" market). By reaching out to our network we found a rep that specialized in connected products. They shared some serious insights about this new market, potential sales channels and what the stores (and the rep) would expect from us in terms of marketing support. We quickly learned even more about how expensive it would be to get our product into stores and we still didn't have an answer for how to build the large number of units that would be required to hit those channels. We really liked this rep firm and wanted to find a way to work with them but they also had a basic retainer fee that we couldn't afford. We felt that they would be a perfect partner to help address our sales shortcomings but we didn't know if we could live up to *their* expectations. It pained us to do it – since it meant more time **not** selling, but we had to say, "We like you but let's talk later."

Around this time, we reached another interesting stage. We started getting phone calls and emails from all of these TV shows around the country. Finally, the major national attention we had been craving. Major media outlets wanted to do feature stories on us. It sounded too good to be true. So we started having conversations with them and then we realized, something didn't smell right. The conversations would turn to all of their viewers and distribution channels and the $20,000 production fee and how many times our segment would air and…. Wait, did you say $20,000? We learned about the paid placement industry. National attention is great but we didn't have those kinds of resources and – even if we did – infomercials did not seem like our best use of funds. We thanked them for their time and moved on.

Emotions: A growing awareness of not knowing what we didn't know.

Lessons Learned: Make sure you find the right partners for sales and marketing and have plenty of conversations before partnering.

Failing Hard at the Penn-Milken Competition
Probably the worst failure to date that we experienced was our visit to the Penn-Milken competition. First off, having gone to the competition was quite rewarding, and we made connections with an incubator called EDSi that eventually expressed serious interest in inviting us to the program. One of the connections we had also led to a great letter of support for our phase 2 grant. The impact that network will have on us is still yet to be seen.

The biggest impact of the trip was learning that we knew significantly little about the education market, and everyone else thought so as well. Although the judges thought TROBO was novel, they did not see how we were going to handle many of the problems we faced in selling a science and math product to pre-K and kindergarten schools. To our significant surprise, although we had a one in five chance of walking away with $20,000 and potentially even $40,000 we walked away with nothing. We were extremely excited, and in our arrogance thought we were a shoe-in for the $40K prize. We didn't even get the crowd favorite vote, which had a $1,000 prize. We were very surprised, because we felt like we gave a very engaging presentation and even have the audience clap and sing along to a TROBO song. But presentation is not everything, and a compelling product that opens doors does not mean you have a product or service that will keep them open.

We learned that time and time again and TROBO has a wonderful curb appeal that get people to come in and look at the product. Unfortunately what we learned is that they might look but they won't buy. Now we're not referring to the specific purchase of a TROBO toy, because we certainly are selling a lot of TROBO toys. They sell very well in the consumer space, because they meet a clear and significant need the parents have to educate children.

However as a business model is concerned, our TROBO educational offering called TROBO EDU, had problems. Some judges told us later that they didn't feel like we had a sales force in place that can handle the work necessary to sell pre-K curricula. Other judges told us the sales cycle was extremely long for kindergarten. We also failed in our presentation to discuss the team of PhDs and teachers that were behind us verifying content and helping us to design the curriculum. That was a standard presentation mistake that we won't make again. So our hopes of landing a critical $40,000, which could've been really powerful for the company were dashed because we didn't have the right answers and we weren't prepared with a presentation directed at that specific audience.

The Penn-Milken experience was definitely a cold shower. But it was necessary, because we learned something very significant about our business plan our business model for TROBO EDU. We learned that although schools thought the toy was novel, they really were more interested in the curriculum and a solution to more pressing problems such as getting financial aid to children in need and improvements on student finance education in general. We also learned another significant problem was that there was less-than-expected demand, because there was no testing required for science and math and pre-K and Kindergarten. Without government-required assessments, it was hard to justify a curriculum that would support science and math. We had spoken about TROBO with several major companies including Houghton Mifflin, Scholastic, etc. all of whom indicated that they were not in a position to try a new technology like the one we had to offer. In general it seems if you do have something that is cutting edge and that is even trying to establish a new market, in our case science and math curriculum for pre-K and kindergarten, people don't see it as an opportunity. Many of them don't see it as an opportunity to do something new; they see it as something that does not fit conveniently in their already busy world. That is perhaps why it is easier to be a really good follower than to be a leader in a new market. Convincing someone that they need something that hasn't existed before is not easy; it requires a lot of salesmanship.

It was an honor to be a finalist in the Penn-Milken business competition, and we learned a lot. But it was almost the psychological nail in the coffin for TROBO EDU. We had to take some time to get away from the competition to absorb the information that was given to us before we could see objectively again. A couple of months later, we began connecting more with locals to the Orlando and Seminole counties, and we realized, the education market is just like any other market. We had to find those like-minded individuals who believe in introducing STEM in early education. That's not going to be everyone. It's not going to be mainstream. It's going early adopters who lead the way, and that's who we're looking for in the education space.

Emotions: We were stunned and disappointed.

Lessons Learned: You are never a guaranteed winner. Stay humble, and always know your audience.

Selling in the Medical Space

We continued to scramble to find revenue for TROBO. From one of our demos, we heard from a parent "My child just had to go into the hospital and she was scared out of their mind. I wish she could have had TROBO to explain what was going to happen to her." In fact, people wanting to put TROBOs in the medical space as a comfort device is a common message we got (and still get). We thought it was a great idea and a great way to use our existing platform – the toy plus the storytelling app – to tell stories about medical procedures and conditions to help make a hospital a little less scary.

We met with several hospitals in the area and they all said we should start in one specific area – radiology. CT scans and MRIs are a reasonably frequent and intimidating procedure. They are also a fairly linear experience – parents and children arrive at the hospital, they check in, they have the procedure and then the doctor reviews the results. The part that is missing is that lying in a loud banging MRI tube for up to an hour can be seriously scary for anyone (especially a child). It seemed like a great opportunity for TROBO.

As we talked to administrators and child-life specialists (incredible people in hospitals who work with children every day to make their experience as relaxing as possible), we learned that the TROBO toy would be a very difficult proposition for a hospital. Due to germs, they couldn't pass it on from child to child and – while we told them they could sell it in their gift shop – it just seemed like they couldn't quite get behind the toy. As difficult as it was to accept (and we had some pretty intense discussions with each other about how we could or couldn't give up the toy), we agreed to explore the idea of just using the app since it was still unique in the hospital environment.

The more we learned about the pediatric hospital environment, we learned that no one was doing what we were proposing. Great news! Finally, recognized problem + TROBO = business opportunity! One fundamental problem kept popping up: who was going to pay for it. The parents would be expected to have a tablet/smartphone and pay for an app to help their children but how would they find out about TROBO. Would the hospital advertise it and try to sell it for us? Alternatively, would the hospital buy it and hand tablets to kids with the appropriate story ready to go? It seemed like a reasonable option given that tablets were already being used in hospitals with kids. We felt like we could easily come up with a subscription amount that would be inconsequential to a hospital but that could be a great recurring revenue opportunity for us.

What we quickly learned was that in a medical system – cost is king. Even if it seems like an insignificant amount, creating a new expense is difficult to push through an organization. Everyone loved what we were trying to do but they couldn't figure out how to pay for it. Like many of the other issues we faced, it would be difficult for us to fund development of vetted medical stories in the hope that hospitals would buy them. But hospitals weren't willing to take a risk that what we would create would be something they could use. After three significant sales efforts complete with proposals, price sheets, and many sales calls, without an active customer, the TROBO medical application began feeling like a distraction from our core STEM business so we had to put it on the shelf.

Emotions: Excitement about a potential market, frustration with a lack of success.

Lessons Learned: Be careful about drowning in opportunity. Look for new business opportunities but see if you can get someone to pay for them first. Put a time/resource limit on how long you are willing to investigate a market, because doing too many things DOES distract you.

Applying for the SBIR NSF Phase II grant

In June 2015, we successfully completed our Phase I SBIR grant with the National Science Foundation. We learned so much about the educational market and demonstrated that – with the accompanying curriculum and teacher tools – TROBO would be a great fit for the early childhood education market. The next step was to apply for the Phase II grant.

The Phase II application is an exhausting process. In addition to demonstrating your successful completion of Phase I, you need to make the business case for your project to demonstrate that the market wants your product. This is easier said than done. You can do research, present interviews and demonstrate that the market is ready for your product but there is no more compelling proof of market demand than a purchase order. But how do you get a purchase order for a product that isn't finished yet? This conundrum exists because the Phase II effort is 2 years long. At the beginning of the process, we didn't have a deliverable product except for our consumer-facing product (the toy plus the storytelling app). But this didn't include the teacher portal, curriculum guides and – most importantly – the full suite of stories necessary to make the complete in-school TROBO experience. So the prospect of getting a PO for a product that was, at-best, a year and a half away seemed impossible. So we had to make the most compelling case we could.

The venue for this case was our Commercialization Plan – a 15-page business plan that included market data, consumer research and other supplementary information to demonstrate market need. In addition, we provided letters of support from industry resources as well as a comprehensive budget and supporting documentation for how we would use the funds over the next 2 years. While the Phase II opportunity would make a huge difference in the TROBO company story, the competition is tough and there is only enough funding for 2 companies in the education space. We put together the strongest application we could, complete with some solid and surprising letters of support, and we crossed our fingers that the NSF sees the value of TROBO in schools for Phase II. As of this publication, we were still several months from hearing the results of our Phase II application. We were told we'd find out in December.

Emotions: Fatigue (we worked around the clock for two solid weeks on the application).

Lessons learned: Start sooner than you think on a grant application. Keep reminding yourself to ask for help even if you feel uncomfortable doing so. People will surprise and support you.

Work/Life Balance – a Perspective by Jeremy Scheinberg

Chris and I have very different perspectives on work/life balance. I have never seen anyone who works as hard and is as driven as Chris is. He has such an amazing set of differing skills that I am constantly amazed with his capabilities. But we have differing outlooks on life and that factors significantly into our work styles.

In my previous career as an engineer for the theme park industry, I traveled a lot. I really enjoyed visiting places all over the world, working on interesting projects. However, that was before I had children. I had resolved to get my work travel out of my system before I had kids because I didn't want to miss a moment with them. When I am away from my family, it is very difficult. At the same time, when I am with them, I don't want to be distracted but that is very difficult for me. By nature, I am someone who is constantly analyzing problems – especially work-related issues – and I have always had problems leaving those thoughts at work. I have resolved to be the best father and husband that I can be because I know that life is short and you don't get those opportunities back. My family is what drives me and I want to make sure I am there for those events – big and small – before my kids grow up (and I know they are growing up fast). Plus, my outlook on TROBO is that if I spent all of my time focusing on a product to make kids' lives better at the expense of my own time with my kids, I would be completely missing the point. We don't get this time back and I want to be there.

When we embarked on this project, my wife Rachel was just returning to work after being at home with our children. Given that she was now going to be the prime breadwinner in the family since we weren't going to be able to draw salaries from TROBO for a while, I took on a greater responsibility for helping out with our children. Rachel's job required her to travel very frequently so – in addition to my day job with TROBO – I was "Mr. Mom." While I was nervous about it at first, I really liked spending time with the kids, taking them to school and picking them up. I would also cook dinner and get them ready for the next day. I wouldn't trade this time with my kids for anything and I was so grateful to Rachel for working so hard for our family. The reality is that TROBO couldn't have gotten to this point without her support.

I know that Chris gives me more credit for having the "balance" part of "Work-Life Balance" down but the reality is that I make a conscious effort to make sure that I don't miss the "life" part and I do my best not to sacrifice that.

Work/Life Balance – a Perspective by Chris Harden

Let me start by saying that Jeremy is much better at work-life balance than I am. He's able to draw boundaries between work and life better than I can. I don't have work life balance; I have work life extremes. In my life, the two times I had the most work life balance are when I work at a company called ADTRAN just out of college, and when I worked at EA SPORTS before starting TROBO. My life generally has been all about work and finding time for my wife Laurie. She's quite tolerant of my need to burn myself out and work more hours than most people, because she understands my life's goal of creating something I can leave behind. Laurie is also familiar with work/life imbalance, because she is a doctor. She went through a rigorous medical program and residency for her M.D.

However even though I do not have life in balance, I do one thing consciously and very well. Laurie and I are in 100% agreement that the time we spend with Asher is golden and to be protected above all else. Therefore when I work more hours than most people, I do not do it by sacrificing Asher's time. I have very clear boundaries around my time that I spend with Asher. As a family we get up in the morning around 6/6:30 we eat breakfast and spend time together before we rush off to school and work. I work all of the day and at roughly five, I head home and I spent all of my attention and time with Laurie and Asher until we put him to bed. At 8:30 or nine I begin work again until usually between midnight and three in the morning. Then I go to sleep and get back up at six or 6:30 and do it all again.

I do this every day of the week including the weekends, except on the weekends I spend more family time, because Asher is not in school. If you're an entrepreneur or perhaps the spouse of an entrepreneur, you will notice something here. You'll notice that I'm not going to bed every night with my wife. There are times where I'm able to do this, so once a week I will in fact go to bed on time, unless I am preparing for something enormous, like being on an episode of Shark Tank. If there are other major deadlines I will go into this mode and not go to bed until the wee hours of the morning.

What does that mean? Yes it is tough on me physically, and it does affect my health. This is something that many entrepreneurs will tell you. Working too many hours does affect your health. The basic tenet of it is your body does its repair work when you sleep. So if you don't sleep, it cannot repair you. But more importantly, the point is that my wife Laurie makes an enormous sacrifice during these periods. She is very tolerant of what we are trying to accomplish with TROBO, as she has been in the past for me with other ventures.

I tend to see the world in terms of resources. We all have access to limited amounts of money, assets like our homes, vehicles and cell phones and other pieces of infrastructure we need to be productive citizens, and as anyone will tell you, *time*. It is the one equalizer among all humans, to my knowledge. I always say to my knowledge, because there are probably at least one or two time travelers who have figured out how to give themselves more time than the rest of us schmoes.

So when I consider that I need to do more work than I am currently doing, my answer to that is I will just sleep less. This is difficult for many people especially those who do not try to create something bigger than themselves. If you are content with life, there is no need to waste extra sleep on doing something more with your life. I am not content with life. I will probably never be content with life, because I see life as a series of plateaus that you leap from to get to the next higher plateau. I see it as a responsibility of mine to God for giving me the opportunity he has given me that I should leap to the next higher plateau. So I sacrificed time by not sleeping.

However I do take time each week to exercise, because I know my machine will not last forever. I try to eat as healthy as I can while trying to gain weight (I'm very skinny) and to stay as healthy as I can for my child and wife.

My biggest concern with my approach work/life extremes is the potential to damage my relationship with Laurie. This is often a common thread with entrepreneurs and their spouses. A workaholic can do long-term damage to the relationship. Being aware of this potential, Laurie and I have a 16-year happy marriage, where we rarely argue, but we do have thorough, thoughtful discussions. Laurie and I consciously communicate regularly about how she's feeling when I am working too many hours, and she is carrying a significant load. Laurie is the quintessential supermom. She not only is a doctor and is currently paying the bills while I go on this adventure with TROBO, she is also a supermom in the sense that she spends enormous amounts of time with Asher, maintains the household, etc. When I am working nonstop hours to drive a big push like the Kickstarter or for Shark Tank, every half-hour I have is dedicated towards those initiatives. I may stop every once in a while to handle trash and dishes, repair some things, etc., but my presence in driving the household diminishes significantly during these dark periods. When this occurs, Laurie ramps up her time maintaining all of this, so that I can go dark and focus on the business. When I come out of the dark period, we balance back out.

This can be difficult because Laurie is very much a fan of real work-life balance and not work-life extremes. However our solid level of communication and honest respect for each other helps us to get through these difficult times, and there are periods where she raises the flag and tells me it is time to dial it back. And I do. It's important if you are going to start your own company that you truly consider whether your significant other can tolerate and support you when you launch the business. And you need to discuss how long will they have to tolerate and support you at these extreme levels of work. Laurie and I seem to have struck a balance where we ebb and flow on this, and as long as I visit the doctor regularly to ensure that I'm healthy, Laurie helps me in every way she can. There are times where I do feel like I'm carrying a mountain, and I know at those times Laurie is carrying an entire planet.

Emotions: Gratitude for your silent partner, your spouse. Constant concern for taking advantage of their support.

Lessons Learned: Pay attention to the journey your significant other is taking with you. Talk often. Dial it back when you need to. NEVER take their contribution and sacrifice for granted.

Partnerships

Starting a company is hard. You never know what each day is going to bring and when it's a small core team, it's almost harder because you feel the entire weight of the business is on your shoulders. There is also this fundamental concern that every decision you make – no matter how big or how small – could be the one that leads to the meteoric success or catastrophic failure of the company. Every day is an adventure and you look for those bright spots to keep you going. Sometimes, it's easy to get so bogged down in the details that you forget to bask in the excitement of what it is you are trying to build. When people tell you that your product is great, you can feel like a proud parent. But sometimes, when they point out issues with your product, it is as if they are calling your baby ugly. That can be hard to take.

It's an emotional journey and it's important to have someone to share it with. You need someone to pull you out of the doldrums on the bad days and to help you celebrate the great days. It's important to prop each other up and that is impossible to do if you are a single founder. It's great to be surrounded by an awesome team but as a founder, there will always be issues that you can't share with anyone else. You don't want to have to be on that island by yourself.

Lessons Learned: Entrepreneurship can be a great (but bumpy) ride. Partners can help smooth out the rough spots.

Enough Planning. Let's Build TROBOs

We had the team in place. We had pre-sold over 500 TROBOs. We had validated the concept and we had tested the educational market. Now, it was time to actually build the toys! In year 1, we had already run our first round of prototypes and in March we successfully manufactured an order of 100 units. All went well.

What Do You Mean It Didn't Pass the Test?

In May, we had begun in earnest to get the "real" production order up and running. But manufacturing, quality control, and compliance testing – which should have been a few weeks ended up taking much, much longer. We knew that our toy needed to be tested to make sure that it met the US safety and compliance rules. When we talked to some of our toy industry experts, they told us that the larger retailers would only recognize one of three major labs – UL, SGS and Intertek. Even though we wouldn't be going into those major retailers from the beginning and we found that there were smaller, cheaper labs out there, we decided would go with one of the big labs. Fortunately, our manufacturer had a relationship with Intertek and they could serve as a liaison between us and the local Intertek office. Testing in China would allow us to keep our costs lower but still give us the testing certificates and prestige of the trusted Intertek name. Our manufacturer coordinated the testing with Intertek and the toy successfully, but slowly completed the testing. There were some complications with the paperwork as much of it was confusing to fill out and – every time we had a question about it – we would lose a day because of the time difference. Plus, even though their English skills were way better than our nonexistent Chinese skills, the language and time differences introduced some delays. But the delays on the plush were not nearly the size of the delays that happened around the FCC certification of our speaker.

From the beginning, we tried to find a speaker that was already certified by the FCC. We knew this would save us time and complication. But no matter how hard we looked, we could not find speakers that met our requirements and were already certified

– even though these speakers can be found on shelves throughout the US. The FCC certification is not a safety certification; it simply says that your device will not interfere with any other devices that might be in similar broadcast frequencies. Since we were using the Bluetooth standard, we weren't overly concerned but we still needed the formal certification.

Intertek ran the first tests and – out of nearly 30 frequencies tested, we failed one frequency by a very small amount and thus failed the entire test. We encouraged our speaker manufacturer to reach out to them to learn more about the failure, which began what would turn into a month and a half delay. Overall, when we combined the slowed communications, time to complete paperwork with everyone, including the FCC, CEC, etc... filings, and the mistakes and retests, we ended up completing all our testing 3 months later than we originally forecast. Although we had not committed to deliver TROBOs until November 2015, we had secretly hoped to deliver them in July. With the 3-month slip, if we were still going to make November, we had no more slack in our schedule for mistakes. This is one of the drivers to our increased shipping costs discussed later in the book.

Emotions: Frustration.

Lessons: Do your homework and make sure you plan ahead when it comes to product testing. Add significant padding in your schedule, if you are a first-timer.

Budget Woes

Creating a budget and then sticking to that budget is something that we expect no one really enjoys doing. We certainly don't enjoy doing it, but we understand it is necessary to do this in order to run the company properly. It's more difficult as a start up to do this, because you often cannot predict your expenses like a mature company that has seen common legal expenses, travel expenses when marketing opportunities arise, shipping expenses when you are desperately trying to make a deadline, and something goes wrong, etc.

One particularly difficult point for us came in September 2015, after the tail end of a tremendously difficult quarter in the history of TROBO. We had been struggling to ship software release 1.2, which was the first time we were able to sell stories, sell a subscription, and use the new username/password mechanism for unlocking our promotional stories in the app that come with the purchase of a unit. In parallel, we had also been battling with getting our manufacturing through safety testing, a difficult coordination with our QA third-party company and vendors, and a seven-day Chinese holiday in October which would eventually delay us by two weeks. In July, we had already completed reinvesting the majority of our grant salaries from the National Science Foundation Phase1 Grant. We were required to take salaries, so we did, paid the income taxes, and then put all of the money back into the company.

We also did the budget at the beginning of Summer 2015 and recognized that we each needed to make reasonable investments to keep the company moving forward ideally through October. We had reviewed the budget and revised it over the summer so we felt pretty good about our estimates. In September we begin to reassess our budget, as we prepared to ship our units. At this point, we were just deciding whether to keep our artists on board or let their contracts finish in hopes of re-hiring them again later. We were evaluating the money we had left to pay our development team in Kosovo, the extra shipping that we were going to have to spend due to having missed our October shipping goals by just a few days, and having to pay four times the amount in shipping to get the units in by November.

A variety of these types of large ticket items came up and our summer budget as well as the fall budget was now looking to be somewhere around $20-$30,000 over our original estimates. That was tough news. We had committed to getting the toys shipped and the mobile app completed before Christmas/Hanukkah, so that we could deliver on our Kickstarter successfully and not let our community down. At this point, the $61,000 Kickstarter project had turned into a project north of $240,000 of real cash invested in the company. This did not include the lost salaries that we had forgone, to work full-time on TROBO.

In September we sat down to review the summer budget and plan fall budget, and we recognized some significant mistakes in our estimates. The significant mistakes tallied up to roughly $20,000. And when we looked at the budget, we also recognized new expenses for fall that did not exist in the summer. As we planned for the company to be announced worldwide with the Shark Tank episode, we knew we would have to move our website, email, etc. to stronger servers. That meant no longer going the cheap route, and instead having to pay monthly fees that were reasonably expensive for a small company. Now looking at another $15,000 each of invested dollars that we would have to put into the company for fall, we felt the impact of what having a poorly developed budget and not having enough capital will do to your company.

For large companies $30,000 is a rounding error. For medium companies it's a negotiating conversation. For a start-up, it could mean the death of the company. We were struggling with two perspectives. The first is "we will do whatever we have to do to get these products out and shipped on time for our November commitment." The opposite extreme was, "we're both at our personal investment ceilings and we will do the minimum necessary to ship a good product, while protecting the rest of our family's savings." At some point the words "money pit" came up for TROBO. It is true, that it had begun to feel like a money pit. We both knew that if something large did not happen for TROBO in the fall of 2015, the company would have to close its doors.

It's interesting. We're sharing this bit of inside information with you, because it is a common theme with startups. There is a concept called "runway". It's an airplane metaphor. Does your company have enough runway to get off the ground? Sometimes it refers to whether or not you have enough distance in front of you to achieve liftoff for your company. In our case, as with many startups, the concept of runway is, "Do you have enough money to last for the time you need to build the company?" We had given the company two years. We had actually given it a year after Kickstarter and had intended to decide whether to keep the company open or close it by the summer of 2015 (and just ship the Kickstarter units). A lot of things have happened however that put that decision into question, such as the potential to get a Phase 2 grant and the potential to be on Shark Tank.

With those large opportunities in front of us, we extended the runway through December. When you are considering whether your company has enough runway to get off the ground, you also have to recognize that the plane is probably getting fatter and heavier as you go. So in the first six months $30,000 would have been a huge help to TROBO. In the last quarter of the year it was just enough to keep us going. And we both knew it was not enough to make the company worth keeping open. So we reviewed the budget. We planned for fall. We committed to a budget that was fixed, with the goal of having a cap on our spending. As much as we both loved it, we knew the spending would have to end, if we could not generate enough sales to make the company healthy.

Coincidentally we were speaking with a friend of ours, who was describing to us how his personal finances had been significantly drained by his start up in the past year. He and his wife had plenty of savings that had been slowly drained by the company, and his team of between 5 to 7 people full-time, are also investing their time and money. He told us that he might close his doors in a couple months if he was not able to land enough sales to keep it open. This seems to be a common theme in many startups: How can you extend your runway? How can you keep from completely draining your own personal savings? We both put our families' financial welfare first. So the decision to finally put a cap on our spending for TROBO was difficult but necessary. The fall of 2015 could very well be the fall of TROBO. We limited our budget, we put our heads down, and we prayed to God for a miracle.

Emotions: fatigue and refocus

Lessons Learned: Be religious about your spending and budget. The little things can add up, and little mistakes can lead to big numbers. Know your spending ceiling, and force yourself to make tough decisions. Your company will be stronger for it.

Shipping Obstacles

When we originally planned our Kickstarter delivery date, we wanted to make sure that we were conservative enough with our promises that we would not miss our date. One recent survey by Professor Ethan Mollick of the Wharton School of Business estimated that 75% of crowdfunding campaigns deliver late. Plus, since many people were ordering them as holiday gifts, we didn't want to miss Hanukkah and Christmas.

When the compliance testing issues pushed back our manufacturing start date past the summer, we decided that we would need to air freight in at least our Kickstarter units instead of shipping them via ocean freight. Our logistics partner estimated that air freight would take approximately 10 days door-to-door versus the 35 days via ocean freight. Plus, we were concerned about any additional complexities that the ocean freight would introduce which could potentially delay delivery even more. The problem was that air freight cost 4 times as much as ocean freight! This wasn't in any of our budgets so it required us to invest even more of our own funds. When we realized that the show could hit before the holidays, we decided to air freight in all of the units. This really killed our budgets but we realized that there was no way we would be able to get the units into the US and then shipped back out in time for the holidays if we went with ocean freight.

We had similar surprise shipping expenses as we did our first rounds of prototypes in China and as we did our first test run of 100 units. Both times the freight added up to hundreds of dollars that we had not anticipated when planning our Kickstarter.

Emotions: Frustration.

Lessons Learned: Shipping expenses can be surprisingly larger than you think, especially if you are manufacturing overseas. They can creep up on you as you make changes to your original plan. Whatever budget you are planning, consider doubling or tripling your expenses as a way to plan for your worst-case scenario.

Shark Tank

While we were working out our manufacturing kinks, we had an interesting opportunity come up, one that could significantly improve TROBO's trajectory.

Applying to Shark Tank
As early as Startup Weekend people have been telling us we should take TROBO onto Shark Tank. Because he doesn't watch TV, Chris confessed he didn't know what the show was until about a year into TROBO. We began the enormous application process including filling out a whopper of an NDA. We shot our pitch video in Chris's house by building a mock stage as close to the Shark Tank stage as we could. We clearly couldn't build the set, but we positioned our product, ourselves, and a big screen TV where we envisioned it would go according to many episodes we watched. We tried to be lively and even opened with a silly joke. We interleaved personal interviews that we shot outside under a lovely shade tree, with a live demo of the toys and the app. For a garage-quality pitch video shot on a couple of consumer cameras and edited with basic software, it came out OK. We submitted and we waited…

During that time, two other reality TV investing show opportunities arose, but we passed on them, hoping to land the big fish. We eventually heard back that we made it to the next level. There were several levels, and we eventually got to go to LA to shoot the episode. Probably the biggest message that kept ringing true from Shark Tank was that there was absolutely NO guarantee we'd be on the show. In fact, even as we write this book, we've not made it on the show. But like in all things TROBO, we try something, and prepare as best we can, in case fate decides to point us in that direction.

While we waited, we trimmed down a 1-minute pitch, and we listened to all the Shark books we could find. We watched as many episodes as we could find. And like anyone who watches the show will tell you, we got our numbers down cold. We read or listened to the books of each Shark – Kevin O'Leary, Robert Herjavec, Barbara Corcoran, Mark Cuban, Daymond John, and Lori Greiner. We were also listening to Zig Ziglar (again). Each book gave us insights into the histories, and passions of the Sharks. We wanted to know how we could identify with them, (*if* we could identify with them). We wanted to know *how* they invested, and how they helped the companies in which they invested. Barbara's was the most creative and story-driven. They spoke about their origins, and we learned not only their stories, but also something powerful. *They all knew how to sell.* The power of this message was resounding. Learn to sell, and you might just succeed. Have the guts to sell, and you will. They all also had one other resounding message – work harder and smarter than your competition while knowing how to sell, and you might just blow the doors off the world. They all did. We recommend reading their books regardless of whether you are trying to get on the show.

The actual taping was a bit of a blur, and we really can't talk about it in detail. The highlights are that it is very intimidating to go into the tank. The Sharks are more intimidating in person, so your time, which goes by in a flash, can be quite draining. We were in the tank for 45minutes, but it felt like 10 minutes. When we were done with the taping, we went back to the greenroom, completely drained from the event. It was a bit surreal, as we still couldn't believe we were even through the process this far. And of course… still no guarantees we'd make it onto the show.

Emotions: Stunned excitement and fear of screwing up.

Lessons Learned: Learn to sell and then do it. Step one in selling, get to know your customer's/investor's/partner's needs. We blew it back in May when pitching a big toy manufacturer; we didn't make the same mistake again when going into the tank.

What if Our Episode Airs?

We had completed our pitch on the backlot of Sony in LA, and we came home hopeful of getting on the show. The Production staff and Legal representatives made it 100% clear that we had no guarantee of being on the show. And we were also under very significant, personal non-disclosure agreements, about even having gone through the Shark Tank process. We couldn't tell anyone without risking a significant lawsuit against our personal finances.

What did it all mean? We might be on a show that has been valued to have about $9M advertising impact for our company. *Holy smokes!!* We knew that potentially hundreds of thousands of people would visit our site the weekend the episode aired. That was the good part, because we had read that many companies sold out of their stock as a result.

The bad part? We knew the episode could air as early as September 25th that summer, or as late as May the next year. We had no guarantee of airing. We couldn't talk to anyone. We had a limited amount of money to spend.

How do you plan for the windfall marketing opportunity of a lifetime on the budget of a startup, not knowing that you will even air, *and* do it without being able to tell anyone? You hedge your bets. You push your own risk tolerance to the limit. And you get your infrastructure ready. You read any tidbit of knowledge blogged by a previous Shark company. You listen to their interviews. We did all of this, and more.

Making TROBOs in volume costs lots of money. Making TROBO's software app costs lots of money in R&D. We knew we had a limited number of units we could afford to make, but if we could just squeeze our wallets a little more, we could take a little more advantage of the opportunity. So we increased our number of TROBOs to 2000 from an initial order of 1000. But when you run the numbers, that's not a windfall. Our problem was the potential to have hundreds of thousands of visitors, which would ideally translate to thousands of orders, and no way to pre-purchase enough stock to fulfill them quickly. We couldn't talk to investors, because we had no guarantee we were getting on the show, oh and of course the NDA was way too scary to consider violating. And that, by the way, seems to be the common problem of anyone lucky enough to get on the show.

We looked at our business model. We had the classic problem of limited stock. We also had access to something similar to Software As a Service (SAAS) in our application. SAAS is basically cloud-based software that allows you to sell it as a subscription. Many of the existing software companies are moving away from a one-time purchase of software to an ongoing subscription. While it might mean less money up front, the opportunity to get a recurring revenue stream is great for a company (and very attractive to potential investors). Up until this opportunity presented itself, we had been going back and forth on whether to allow customers to buy TROBO stories without buying the toy. We had proforma income statements for the next three years, and we could see how powerful the install base of many TROBOs could be in driving sales. On the other hand, we had seen other scenarios where allowing app sales that weren't limited by TROBO units were compelling too. If people came to our site, and they could not buy a TROBO, they could at least buy a story. And like SAAS, the number of stories that could be bought was limitless. We weren't capped because we couldn't afford to buy units.

So we made the decision to allow app sales without TROBOs. This immediately begs the question, "Why do I need the TROBO, if I can buy stories without it?" First, the unit adds the emotional connection and interaction with the app that will encourage a stronger love of learning as the TROBO toy reads the story to the child. That has never changed. The financial value is that customers who buy the toy get their first 5 stories for free. They really *are* for free, because our margins are so low on the toys.

Anyone who sells items in retail will confirm just how difficult it is to make money in retail with low volumes. The strain is even worse in toys, as they are often viewed as a commodity.

To prepare the app, we focused the team on accelerating the next release for early September just in case we aired as early at 9/25. We buckled down and booked more hours of work time. We thought about other ways supporters could buy, even if we sold out of TROBOs. We began to view the Shark Tank opportunity as our Kickstarter campaign on steroids. What other things could we make available that didn't have 3months lead-time? We got our coloring book done early, which is print-to-order with a lead-time of 2 weeks or so. We put smaller stories into production, including converting the shark story that we built especially for the show into a short story. It turned out really cute, by the way. And frankly, we wrote this book for that purpose too.

People often ask us to tell our story. We are in the Kickstarter company mindset of sharing all the behind-the-scenes. As entrepreneurs who were interested in Kickstarter, we read and listened to all we could to learn how to have a successful Kickstarter. We did the same for the grant and for Shark Tank. We read all the Shark's books. If there was a company who wrote a book on how their experience was before or after Shark Tank, we would have read it. So we think others who see Shark Tank may be interested in hearing what we are going through. It's important to "Pay it Forward."

We also decided that there was no driver to sell TROBO through retail outlets this year. Hoping that we would be lucky enough to sell out of our limited stock and knowing how much margin it costs to be on retail shelves, we pivoted for this year. We moved to Shopify – an online e-commerce platform that allows you to more easily build a website with online ordering capabilities (instead of developing everything yourself from scratch). Plus, Shopify is a very well known company that we felt we could trust to keep our website up and running even if we received a huge surge in traffic due to the show airing. We moved our email to Rackspace – a very robust web/email provider for the same reason.

We planned a small budget for SEO and other online marketing, and we got back to our Kickstarter roots of regular blogging, podcasts, interviews, and other grass-roots efforts. Or goal is to drive online sales through grassroots marketing and hopefully make it onto the show.

Now this all sounded well and good until the Development team all planned to take August vacations. In late July, every developer on our team told us they were taking vacations just as we were planning to announce the R1.2 release effort in prep for the 9/25 Shark Tank season premiere. We struggled. Here we needed our entire team to double-down, and we couldn't tell them why. And they were planning to take surprise simultaneous vacations. We did something we've never done in our entire management careers; we asked them to delay their vacations. We explained something big was coming, and provided a goal date, but we couldn't say why. We asked them to trust us. *And they did.* It's the first time we've understood why someone may be so desperate that they ask you to delay a vacation. Ownership of a company sometimes means asking for favors, and in this case, even begging. *Yes, we begged.* You make a trade off even when you go against your personal values on how to treat people. Just be aware that you should only do it when absolutely necessary.

Emotions: We had a lot going on without knowing if/when things might hit. While the opportunities were certainly exciting, waiting was pretty overwhelming.

Lessons Learned: Opportunities present challenges to how you run your business. Be willing to pivot. And sometimes be willing to ask for help when you really need it.

Keeping the Cat in the Bag

We had a bizarre thing happen with the opening of the Shark Tank season. We were briefly featured on the trailer for Shark Tank. It was a 2 second sound bite. Though one might consider this a nod that we were going to be on the show, we'd seen enough movie trailers to know that just because something is in the trailer, it does not mean it will be on the show. We were initially thrilled but soon reminded ourselves that we had no guarantees of being on the show. And our NDA was still in place, which meant we still had to keep quiet.

Of course, we found out about it when a friend of TROBO tweeted it to us 3 weeks before the season premiere. Fortunately the tweet didn't last long, and we didn't answer. We took the approach of not answering anything like that online. A few days later, a friend in our co-working space called us out on it. Over the week or two after the premiere, we received a handful of offline Facebook messages, emails from old friends, and people pulling us aside on the co-working space asking if we were going to be on the show. By the 2nd week of October, we had complete strangers asking us about it. We regularly talked about not going to Canvs, just to avoid the potential of further leaks. Our biggest concern was that one of our significant influencer friends would tweet about it, and we wouldn't be able to reel it back in. We also wanted to make sure we didn't violate our NDA, but the second concern was losing the buzz around our announcement, if we ever got on the show.

So how did we handle it? Very early, we began rehearsing a standard line that we could not confirm what they had seen on TV, and that we had heard participants on the show were required to sign a hefty NDA. That worked well as most people just wanted to celebrate but stayed professional about not probing. Many already knew about the kinds of NDAs in reality television shows. At some point we realized this was an interesting challenge that every company featured in the trailer was going through and wondered how they were handling it.

Emotions: An ambivalent mix of excitement and stress

Lessons Learned: Keeping a potentially huge piece of information bottled up is difficult in the Information Age. You can't control what is going to air and – once the genie is out of the bottle – it's really hard to put it back in. You gain respect for the enormous amount of pressure reality TV shows' participants are under. If you're a friend of someone who participates on a reality TV show, be cool about probing or publicly celebrating until THEY have announced it.

They're Here!!!

Finally, in the middle of October, our first shipment of TROBOs arrived in the US. It was an incredibly exciting moment, although we were very anxious as we got limited information about where exactly our shipment was. It ended up getting put on a truck once it reached the US – even though we paid for it to be shipped by air! But once that truck showed up, it made everything more certain. We had case after case of Newtons and Curies all boxed up. All we had to do was put in the manuals (they had the unique codes that allowed TROBO buyers to get their stories) and ship them out to our Kickstarter backers.

We looked at many of the fulfillment options out there and – in order to save some money and preserve our margins – we decided to fulfill the Kickstarters and the first batch of orders ourselves. From Chris's garage we set up an assembly line to fulfill orders from Shopify through a shipping solution calling ShipStation which integrated with our website. As we moved through our Kickstarter shipments – and as new orders came in – we could easily fulfill the orders in the system, print out shipping labels and send them on their way. The toughest part was fitting all of the TROBOs in our cars for their trip to the post office. We looked at other options including UPS and FedEx but – in our case – Priority Mail was cheaper and faster and since every dollar counts, we went with that option. The great part about ShipStation was that we could look at the shipping costs for each individual shipment and go with the best option for each box.

For our Orlando Kickstarter backers, we decided to bring them their TROBOs personally. Yes, it was probably inefficient but it really felt good to meet the people who had supported us when we needed them most, look them in the eyes, and say "Thank You." Yes, it was a tough road to get to that point, but when we saw the excited children (and parents!), it was all worth it.

User Trials - Over 1000- and No Sign of Stopping

In October 2015, at a convention in Orlando called OiX, we hit our one-thousandth product demo. As of the writing of this book the TROBO concept is a year and three quarters old. We have performed over 1000 user trials and demonstrations to children, parents, retailers, buyers, distributors, etc. We have performed them in conventions, at our homes at our co-working space, at many random places. Anywhere and everywhere there was an opportunity to present a demo we did it. This is especially true during our Kickstarter, where we both took the mantra, "TROBO - never leave home without it." We had TROBOs in our cars and iPads paired with them at the ready in case someone showed interest and wanted a demo.

After a while we developed a friendly competition. We purchased hand counters that fit in your palm with a little button to increment a number. We have two of them that we take to conventions and trade shows. At a given show like ISTE we would go back-and-forth sharing the opportunity to do demos and user trials with people who would visit our booth. And we would enjoy the opportunity to have beaten the other with the number of demos that we perform. We decided to purchase the handheld counters when we started losing track of the specific numbers at a given convention. We wanted to ensure that when we said we had done 600 demos, 700 demos, 800 demos etc. that we were being accurate representation of those numbers. The counters cost a dollar and a half each but they allowed us to accurately track the number of demos and user trials that we performed and to have fun during the process.

With 1000 user trials so far, we've heard nearly all the complaints and questions and concerns that come up when one reviews the product. However we continue to do them, because we are always developing new content. New content being new stories, new user interfaces, new puzzles etc. that must be put in front of people customers children etc. outside of our own company, so that we don't mistakenly build the wrong experience.

It is these demos that drive the product changes that we make. Our parental focus group and our Kickstarter groups still help us to guide the overall product development and a customer community driven fashion, but it is these hands-on experiences, watching and keeping our mouths shut, asking frank questions of retailers and buyers, and other user's parents etc., that determine the subtleties of the product that make it feel polished and professional. If you're not forcing yourself to watch someone use your product while you say nothing, you should do it. It is always difficult and uncomfortable, but you gain so much. This coming year as we hope to begin development of TROBO EDU, we will be putting the devices into pilot programs with prekindergarten and kindergarten schools. That promises to be a lot of fun, because of every user trial we'll get to add 20 or 30 students to our number of demos, and more importantly we get their feedback, which will help guide the future of the product and our services.

Emotions: Nervous fun

Lessons Learned: Let customers tell you what is good and bad with their actions. Look for large trends in the feedback, not one-offs.

Starting Year 3: Selling, Retail, and TV

The 2015 Holidays – a Roller Coaster of Emotions

Wrapping Up Kickstarter
We were excited to deliver our Kickstarter and Tilt preorders and kept busy during the first 20 days or so shipping units and trying many times to reach some of the backers who never answered their emails to get addresses. (Kickstarter doesn't give you addresses; you ask once you are ready to ship.) That was wonderful. Then things got tough.

Sorry, No More Grant Funding

Late in November just before Thanksgiving we were notified by the NSF that we would not be getting the Phase II grant. Although we were certainly hopeful, we knew it was a real possibility that we wouldn't be chosen.

So at this point, just before Thanksgiving, we had delivered on Kickstarter early (yay!), and lost our Phase II grant opportunity (boo!). This meant we were free to start selling as hard as we could, and we were no longer going to pursue the Education market. The first item is obvious, and we'll talk more about that in the next chapter The last, that we were not going to pursue the Education market, was actually kind of relieving. We had been told in the past to focus on doing one thing extremely well as a startup, but we hadn't. In the past year we pursued the Medical market, Education market, and Consumer (or Retail) market. As a startup, you are always looking for what is going to bring in revenue and you tend to focus on that. While we were initially focused on Retail, we felt (and we kept hearing from people) that Medical and Education "would be great markets for TROBO." So we had to at least take a look. As we mentioned, Medical didn't pan out and now Education was going to be difficult since it would require so much upfront investment and – without the grant – we wouldn't have the resources to fully develop a product for schools. We were now free to just pursue the Retail market. We were now finally able to say, "no, but thank you" to anyone pitching us on the idea of our pursuing institutions. It would have been nice to have the Phase II grant though; no denying it.

Emotions: This was a dark month for us, even though we had made it to the "first finish line".

Lessons learned: Sometimes when a door you wanted open actually closes, it's not necessarily a bad thing, though it may feel like that at the time.

Black Friday and the Content Marketing Learning Curve

The week before Thanksgiving, we had a scary epiphany. Black Friday was less than a week away and we had NO plan. The absolute biggest sales day (or weekend) in the year, and we had nada. We had been so focused on delivering our Kickstarter units, we had not done anything in prep. We started sweating.

The first thing we did was apply to Amazon Marketplace. It took a few hours, but we got Curie on there. Then in trying to duplicate her and make Newton we fowled something up that would come to bite us about 2 weeks later. Once we got Curie up, we focused on our own site and marketing plans. We went full force with "content marketing", which essentially meant we'd blog each day and post links on all social media as well as buy ads on most SEO systems and social media. We also created our Black Friday and CyberMonday discount codes and plastered the site and social media with ads.

Each night we write up a new blog. We chose or created an image that was hopefully eye catching, and we put anywhere from $5 to $20 on the ad. We started out with these ad areas:
- Retargeting
- Google Adwords
- Facebook Ads
- Twitter

We'd be up until about 1 or 3 every night from that Monday before Black Friday through the end of Cyber Monday. At the end of the day we'd use the Shopify dashboard to see which ads or blogs drive the most traffic to our site. We'd try our best to read the statistics each site offered for impressions, budget spends, click-throughs and then, finally, costs-per-click.

Each night, if something wasn't working, we'd redirect money to the ones that were working. We found that Twitter was charging us $20 per day for impressions with zero click-throughs. After 2-3 days we pulled their budget and put it into Facebook and Google. About half way through we realized that the retargeting campaign (which focused on the approximately 11K visitors who previously came to our site) was also charging for a low amount of impressions and with literally less than 10 click-throughs, charged us about $3 per click-through. After a couple of technical debacles where we could not get support quickly (we think they are in India which introduced a significant delay), we stopped the retargeting campaign and funneled that money into Facebook and Google.

We also learned that (except for Twitter), it was actually HARD to spend the entire budget allocated for a given ad. We were building up a surplus of unspent dollars. So each night, in addition to redirecting money from failing advertising channels, we'd skim off the extra budget from ads that weren't spending their entire budget and funnel that into winning ads on Facebook and Google. In the end, we spent most of our funds (and got solid results) on Facebook ads and Google Adwords. We also learned that these systems are extremely powerful (and complex) and we could see how a full time person could be needed to run these SEO and Ad systems for a company.

We also established stores on Pinterest and Facebook, to see if convenience of buying while in Facebook would have an impact. They did not convert to any sales.

Alas, with all of our hard work, we felt like we had failed for Black Friday and Cyber Monday. We didn't see the sales we had hoped to. We learned later after talking with two mentors from the toy industry that we didn't do half bad. We ended up with a conversion rate of about 1.5 to 2%. That means for every 100 visitors to the site, 1 or 2 would buy. Apparently getting to 4% is considered doing really well. But combining that mediocre performance with the fact that the show had not aired (and apparently wasn't going to) before Christmas, we were very concerned that our holiday sales numbers were going to look ridiculously low in January. That would make it hard to pitch any investors or even buyers from large retail chains. But then a small miracle happened…

Xploration Station

We learned a ton during our Black Friday balderdash, but the main thing we learned was that we'd perform ok in sales, if we could just get people to our site. However, our biggest problem was actually getting people to our site. Enter Fox TV and XplorationStation. XplorationStation is a nationally syndicated television show for early teens about cool technology. They had interviewed TROBO a couple of months earlier and aired our episode the week after. They aired to 80 stations across the country from that Friday to Sunday. They did a wonderful piece on us and drove thousands of visitors to our site that weekend, which was amazing and validating. We offered a smaller discount than we did for Black Friday to celebrate XplorationStation, and many people took advantage of it. We learned a few things that weekend.

First at one point our conversion rate was up to 1 in 7 people; this further validated that people would buy TROBO. In an effort to grow our SKU count from just two TROBOs, we had also added a personalized adoption certificate and a coloring book. There were tons of people who bought the entire TROBO experience. We had often been told our price point of $70 was too high, but with these customers, who reached close to $100, we confirmed that people would invest that much in their children, if we could show them the value. We were also thrilled that our small add-ons were generating more revenue for our tiny company and more value for our customers.

Second, we got a trial run of what the Shark Tank weekend run would be like. We got emails, phone call orders, Twitter, questions from our website forms, and Facebook messages. They came in quickly, and we answered just as quickly. We ended up building templates of all the common questions, so that it became a simple copy and paste to address them.

Third, we fixed a mistake that we made in the Black Friday weekend. We had forgotten to put an "intent marketing" survey on the site to ask customers why they were not buying TROBOs when they left the site. We put a free trial plugin into Shopify and as the thousands of people came through we gathered their reasons for not buying. The two largest responses we got were that we didn't support their platform (Android) or the price was too high. We had also offered "I don't understand how TROBO works" and "I'm not impressed with TROBO" as other answers, which barely registered. There are more lessons we can take away from the survey, one being that we can write blogs that are better targeted to those who would buy TROBO, which should increase our conversion rate.

Amazon Marketplace and the weeks before Christmas

For the next couple weeks leading up to Christmas we kept up or content marketing efforts, putting out a blog every couple day and placing ads driving traffic to the blog. The blog had ads embedded for TROBO. This worked well enough.

We also saw steady sales of Curie TROBOs on Amazon during the period leading up to Christmas, even when we had discounts on our own site. Some customers either only found us through Amazon or decided they preferred to buy from the trusted retailer more than us. We were happy either way, but there was one problem. We learned that Amazon has rules about how long your toy or store has to be listed on the Marketplace before the holidays to be allowed to sell your toy during the holiday season. They try to protect their customers from a bad experience if a young manufacturer (like TROBO) can't handle the heavy volume or tight shipping deadlines of Christmas. And although we were lucky enough to have Curie stay on the store and sell (quite well), Newton TROBO was flagged and delisted. We went back and forth over email, but we were never able to get them to relist Newton until January.

Emotions: Stress from an extremely high learning curve in a short time. Gratitude to XplorationStation's team for believing in us.

Lessons learned: Figure out your SEO and marketing plans well ahead of your sales cycle's peak season. The absolute best way to learn about SEO, ads, driving traffic, etc… is to just do it. Spend a little money and see what works for you on the different platforms.

2016 – A New Year

We were exhausted in December and took the last week and half to do non-TROBO things (besides customer support of course). In December we were lucky enough to meet with Qubits toys, who are also in Orlando, and they have become a mentor. Mark (the owner) put us in contact with Amazon's Exclusives group. We applied, were accepted, and began the ramp up process for Fulfilled By Amazon (FBA). Over the month we shipped units to Amazon, filled out our special content section for the Exclusive products, and became an official Amazon Exclusives partner. That means we only sell TROBOs through them and through our website, and in exchange for a smaller percentage than what retail normally takes, they handle all the shipping and marketing to drive sales on Amazon for us. (We can still run ads of course.)

We also wrote our first trade paperback for children 6-9, developed the next round of myPal TROBO Personality Panels for a new release, and completed the storyboards for a new story coming out in March. Looking back we had a strong holiday cycle, and we're now generating income for the company from sales. We're working on new items for our customers based on their requests, including getting quotes for porting our app to Android.

Amazon Exclusives

The choice to join Amazon exclusives turned out to be a great one. Once we got all of the "A+ content" in place, as they call it, we began to see an interesting shift in buying behaviors. Although our site traffic remained steady, nearly all of our orders came from Amazon FBA. Our sales from Shopify nearly dried up, as every one was buying from Amazon. They provided a steady stream of orders, which was wonderful, because this allowed us to focus more on execution of content, prototypes, company business, and less on Marketing. Although we still did some content marketing, the real benefit we saw in joining Exclusives was that they were doing a much more effective job of marketing than we could. We are two guys. They are Amazon. It's kind of a no-brainer. We also repacked our 10 unit boxes to match their *very-specific* specifications. FBA does have guidelines, and they can be intimidating, but once we got past the learning curve, it became very comforting to be a part of the FBA and the Exclusives program.

The first thing we learned is that Amazon gets insanely cheap shipping rates. For us to ship a TROBO using US Priority mail, it is around $10 on average. For us to ship a box of 10 TROBOs to Amazon, it also costs $10. So, although they take a bit more margin for their marketing and FBA efforts, it becomes a real savings on the shipping side of things. It is also wonderful to ship a few cases every few weeks to Amazon instead of individual units to the same number of customers all over the country. That confirmed what we had been told by other vendors, which was it would again freed us up to focus on other things. Exclusives seems to really take care of their vendors; at least they have so far with us. We are now into March as of the time of this writing, and they have consistently provided steady sales.

The only downside was that some of our add-on products weren't getting the additional exposure, so we eventually took steps to get our coloring book onto Amazon using Createspace in hopes of getting some of those sales back.

Our next step was to pitch Amazon on including us in their STEM section. That has yet to come to fruition, but our fingers are crossed.

Emotions: Elation that taking the leap into FBA and Exclusives was the right choice for us.

Lessons learned: We might be a couple years into this, but it still pays off to take risks, even if it is just to learn about how something works.

Shark Tank – We get the Golden Ticket!

One Friday night late in March, we received a very exciting email from one of the Shark Tank Producers. The subject line told us the airdate. We called each other to celebrate and plan for the weekend. Suddenly everything about our dreams for the show became REAL. Months earlier we had planned everything out (see earlier section). Then, as time wore on, and we heard nothing, our spirits began to drop. With each passing week, we saw our hopes change from "We've GOT to air" to "well, I don't know", to "did you read the TV Guide listings this week? No I forgot."

Rightfully, our attention had already been refocused back on every other iron we had in the fire. We had moved ahead assuming we wouldn't get on the show, but we were still hopeful. That may seem like the obvious decision, but as mentioned earlier, we were initially quite tempted to "sit on" our TROBO units waiting for the big news, not trying to sell them into retail. This would have meant not doing cold calls in November trying to get buyers to let us into last minute retail sales, not scrambling over the holidays to make discounted sales in Black Friday, and not joining Amazon exclusives either. Why would we have been tempted to do this? The general story one hears when listening to product companies who have gone through the Shark Tank experience, is that they will run out of stock. We heard that hundreds of thousands of visitors will come to their site and buy product. If we held on to all that stock, we wouldn't have to share any margin with any retailers. The gamble in doing this of course was that our episode may not have aired, and we'd have ended up with lots of inventory and no established sales channels.

As timing had it, in November we eventually learned our episode wasn't going to air before Christmas & Hanukkah, so we punted on sitting on the units. That's a dangerous way to run a company anyway, so we began selling on Amazon, and per the previous section, that worked out well. We've learned a ton about the retail space in exchange for a bit of invested time, hustle, and some margin.

By the time we received the news in March, the task list we built in September had gone stale. We had to freshen it up. We met the following morning and rebuilt it according to the company's latest priorities for moving forward. Our rollout plan was moving ahead, and over the next three weeks (which is how long we had until the show aired), we were be heads-down getting as many pieces in place as possible for the show. What does a company do to prepare for the coming "Shark Tank Tsunami"? For us this meant, among many things:

- Pushing one more story to the app store (our Mars story). The eBooks had no limit on inventory, so one more story meant that many more potential sales.
- Finishing off this book. Our goal to have this as print-to-order and more importantly as a Kindle book was another eBook without inventory limits. As important, we hoped that some SharkTank visitors may not have a need for a TROBO, but they may have an interest in our journey and thus pick up the book.
- Asking for advice from advisors who we couldn't contact before (due to confidentiality limitations)
- Finding friends to help us man the phones, email, and social networks for the big night
- Centralizing scripts/canned responses to our most frequently asked questions from potential customers, so our friends could quickly answer the deluge of questions we anticipated the night of the airing
- Setting up a phone service to help with the anticipated call volume. We knew some customers would still be interested in phone orders, so we rented a virtual assistant phone service.
- Finding friends to help us ship for the big weekend
- Sending press releases. These were prepped and waiting.
- Sharing the news with everyone who knew about TROBO
- Prepping our remaining inventory and supplies (unboxing cases into individual units for fulfillment the weekend the show hits)
- Prepare "sold out" messaging for the website and choosing a refill date for Amazon stock. As much as we would have

loved to have so much inventory that we wouldn't sell out, we didn't have the funds to buy that much inventory. And again, it was too much of a gamble to buy that much inventory with no guarantee of airing
- And about 30-40 other minute details

Emotions: An emotional bottom as the end of Shark Tank season 7 approached. Absolute excitement upon the news. We'd been given the golden ticket, and it was time to execute our plans. There WAS some physical dancing that took place – with our wives, not each other.

Lessons: Stay focused on your business. If you get an unlikely chance at something big, prepare as much as you can. Just don't bank on it.

After the Tank

By now, you have probably seen our episode of Shark Tank. Yes, the show that we worried might never aired was finally shown on April 8, 2016. We got an email from Sony and ABC 3 weeks before our episode was due to air. We were feeling pretty low at that point. There were less than 6 weeks of episodes left in the season and we were starting to feel as if our episode was probably not going to make the cut. We were feeling disappointed because we had this humongous secret that we couldn't tell anyone yet it had the potential to make such a big impact on our tiny little company.

When we finally got "the email" we went back to our task list to implement our "STAir" plan. All along, we had been referring to the show by the code "ST" so we could talk about it amongst ourselves but (hopefully) no one else would know what we were talking about. Our STAir plan included tasks such as notifying press, our respective universities, Shopify and other online service providers that we used so they could be ready for the inevitable flood of traffic. A friend who had been on the show told us that there was a secret online group for Shark Tank alumni. He invited us to the group and we immediately began posting questions.

Everyone on the group was incredibly friendly and supportive. We also reached out to TJ Hale from the Shark Tank Podcast and Neal Hoffman from Mensch on a Bench. They were both awesome and gave us some great advice about PR and long range planning. Both of them stressed the need to extend the "Shark Tank Effect" from one night to multiple months. This could be done by hiring a PR person and – most importantly – for installing mechanisms on our website that would allow us to capture emails – of both customers and people who just stopped by to look – in order to communicate with them about our progress and potential upsell opportunities. Over the course of the next week and a half, we spoke to representatives from ActiveCampaign (a very intelligent email marketing/targeting platform), RevenueConduit (a SaaS product that connects Shopify with ActiveCampaign) and Privy (a plugin for Shopify that allows us to incent people to share their email address). After much scrambling (and with some great support from the three companies), we got their systems installed and configured and felt that our capture mechanisms were ready to go. One additional complication was our inventory situation. We were limited on inventory so we had to decide how much inventory to ship to Amazon. This was complicated because Amazon was doing such an awesome job of promoting our product but our margin was much better on our own website. Since we were limited in inventory, every penny of margin was critical (we were going to use those funds to reinvest in new content and new units). In the end, we elected to send them a portion of our inventory but keep the lions' share for us to fulfill.

We realized we needed help with our social media the night of the airing. One of our good friends, Josh Murdock (who had been there the day TROBO was born at Startup Weekend and whose son Jack was our first TROBO "validator") volunteered to be our "Social Media Captain". He assembled a team of other Friends of TROBO – Bess Auer, Necole Pynn, Diane Court and Melissa Wasserman – to help take over our social media team up to (and including) our airdate. They did a great job of rallying support to TROBO and getting people excited for our episode.

Finally, we needed a party. Yes, it's no fun watching yourselves on Shark Tank alone so we asked our friends at Canvs – Melissa Wasserman and Shanika Marlow – if they would help throw a

"Shark Tank Watch Party" for us. They graciously accepted and put together an awesome party with a great crowd.

The Show
So now that you have seen the show, you know what happened. We made our pitch and did a demo with Daymond John that was really cute. After taking some tough questions about the product's price, Mark Cuban, Daymond, Kevin O'Leary and Lori Grenier went out in rapid succession. That's at least how it looked in the 8 minute cut of the show. Behind the scenes we were in the tank for 45 minutes, where we covered much more information than was shown on the episode (see below). During the taping, only Lori went out right after Daymond. Before Robert could give his response, Chris interrupted him and asked if he could share his own story. Chris shared his difficult background and the value that his mother placed on education. Robert shared his own background and the common ground they both had. Robert recognized the value of our app/toy platform and proposed a potential partnership with DreamWorks Animation. Contingent on making a deal with DreamWorks, Robert agreed to a deal for $166,000 in return for 1/3rd of the company. We accepted, shook hands and hugged. Just when things weren't looking good for us, we made a deal. At the time, we were hopeful that a partnership with Robert – as well as our emotional story – would help our episode to air (only 80-100 of the 130 companies they tape actually make it to air!) We had beaten over 100,000 applications for season 7 to get to this moment; it was truly exciting.
As we sat in the Watch Party, we knew the outcome but no one else did. When Robert agreed to the deal, the crowd roared. It was an amazing feeling to be able to share that with our friends and family.

What You Didn't See On TV
After the elation of being on Shark Tank died down a little, we reflected on our taping experience versus what aired on TV. We

quickly realized from talking to family and friends that we were in a little bit of trouble. We had taped over 45 minutes in Los Angeles but – given that all of the segments need to be edited down to 8 minutes – we knew that much of it would be cut. Unfortunately, several critical elements of our story were left on the cutting room floor. If you had never heard of TROBO before Shark Tank, you would never know that:

Chris and Jeremy were both former theme park and video game engineers.
We had experience in storytelling and creative development.
We were both fathers to little kids.
We were both frustrated by our kids' mindless toys.
There is a lack of quality STEM education toys for kids 2-5.
TROBO has a variety of amazing personalized stories that are available in the app that help kids learn about science, technology, engineering and math.
Kids love TROBO and we had done almost 1000 demos at the time to prove it.

Unfortunately, all of that was lost in the edit. It really felt like a missed opportunity to get kids, parents, and retailers excited about TROBO and its educational potential. Instead the show seemed to fixate on price, which varies based on quantity. We had discussed getting the price down below $50 when the quantities were higher, but that was also cut.

After The Show
So maybe you saw the show, maybe you didn't. You can usually find it on youTube. But here's what happened afterwards…
Two weeks after the show, we were contacted by Robert's team to begin the due diligence process. Of the deals that are consummated on the show, only 25% go from handshake to an actual transaction. Even though our deal was a contingency deal (no agreement with DreamWorks, no $166,000, no 33% equity), we wanted to work with Robert and make things happen. We can't go into all of the details as we signed an NDA with Robert's company, but they performed a detailed review of our financials and our business model. There were some items in their agreement that we weren't thrilled with and they probably wanted our financials to look a

little better (at this time we were still pre-sales; our units wouldn't arrive from China until the end of October and the holiday season is where we knew the real action was).

At the end of October we received an email from Robert's group that told us they would not proceed with investing in TROBO after all. They were extremely professional, and we are grateful to Robert and his team for giving TROBO a chance. The day we got the news, of course it was tough. That night, Chris went out on his back porch, sat in silence, and just thought about the future of the company. Even Asher who was 3+ at the time noticed something was wrong and asked. He gave him a hug and said it would get better. That was a tough blow, but apparently it is pretty common. There are just too many things that affect a deal that are never aired on TV.

The Final Year of TROBO

After the SharkTank episode ran, things began to fall apart for TROBO. We had hoped to sell out of units, raise another round of funds, and build TROBO 2.0. What actually happened was hard, drawn out, and simply took time to play out. In many ways it mirrored the Kübler-Ross model, widely known as the "five stages of grief" (Denial, anger, bargaining, depression, acceptance) one goes through when someone they love dies. That sounds a bit melodramatic, but bear with us. The dying of a business can be quite comparable to the dying of a loved one. Some models have seven stages, where "shock and denial" is the first stage. That probably best matches what we experienced the night of and the month after the airing of the Shark Tank episode.

Our local community celebrated our accomplishment with us at a party the night of the episode. Unfortunately, the show focused on price, which played a large factor in the purchasing decision when people visited our site. We had not reached the volumes necessary to drop to the price recommended on the show, so we had a remarkably low level of sales. People even emailed us frustrated messages asking why we hadn't dropped the price. Although the show does a wonderful job of promoting the exciting things about entrepreneurship, it just doesn't have time to educate its audience on how businesses must price their products to make money. And in the end, our constant struggle to make an Internet of Things (IoT) tech toy that was also plush simply failed. Whether it was Kevin O'Leary on Shark Tank, a panel of representatives we met at Target, or even a friend wishing to buy out TROBO at the end, the constant pressure we experienced was to get TROBO to less than $30. That was only achievable in volumes we never figured out how to reach.

In the following months, the writing on the wall became clearer and clearer for us. Both of our financial runways had come to an end. Jeremy began to see no way to continue without further financial investment. Chris's second child was on the way which would significantly change his financial landscape. Both wives, who had been extremely supportive, began to have doubts as well.

We all knew by this point the way the hard part of the toy business works. Essentially as a product producer with a seasonal product (like toys, for example) you have to pay for manufacturing roughly in March and plan for your shipments to be available to retailer warehouses by July. Then you have to wait until late November, and December to see what your sales will be, and then get paid in January (30—90 day terms, depending on the retailer). If things sell well, you do it all again struggling to stay in business during the low season until the holidays hit again and investing even more in next year's manufacturing to grow your footprint. If sales don't go well, you get a lot of returns from retailers, don't get the income, and you may be stuck with a lot of inventory. So you do what many toy manufacturers do and cut your prices to just above wholesale in the holidays just to get out what you put in and clear out inventory. That's where Black Friday sales come from.

During our run we made several friends who had significant financial disasters while trying to make their toy businesses stay alive year to year, and it seemed the more successful they got, the larger the risk they had to take each year. As parents, we did not feel taking that much personal financial risk was the best decision for us.

So we tried to partner with investors. April through June, we met with several in the central Florida area, networking with good friends we had built along the way. We also met with a Chinese investor in California. And we reached out to an old friend and mentor of Chris's who was an investor. Each time we heard tough versions of the same news – the business model we had was broken. It was not an investable company, even with the TROBO

2.0 hardware and branding concept we prototyped and built into our pitches. Every investor was friendly, but they all echoed the same concern that we couldn't get the volumes high enough to generate a 10x return on their investment. The 10x return conversation is a pretty common expectation, and although most expect more like a 3-5x return, most investors want to see that you can at least demonstrate a viable shot at it. Frankly, we couldn't.

One local investment organization did still believe in TROBO. The Firespring Fund, a second stage fund, had offered to have us join their entrepreneurial class with a convertible note as the seed funding of something around $30K. However they had a start date coming up quite soon that summer, and we were starting to lose faith in the business's ability to scale without help. So we gave ourselves a deadline. If by a month before the class started, we could find future investors who would invest in us after graduating from Firespring, we'd join their first class. If we couldn't find strong indication from future Venture Capitalists (VCs), we wouldn't join Firespring, because another startup could take our place and use that funding to grow.

We didn't want to take their investment just to languish a few more months, and we didn't want to rob another startup of the chance to grow unless we knew we could achieve investment later. And we didn't want to be a small, struggling family business with an enormous amount of financial risk with little to no margins.

In June we declined the Firespring offer, thanked them, and setup about winding down the company. Jeremy soon went to work at Universal Parks & Resorts full time. Chris had his second child, Finley, and he went back to Electronic Arts. We continued to build content for the app store and promoted selling the rest of the stock.

That November we had earnest discussions with a friend of ours who really understood how to make inroads into retail. We discussed him taking over the brand we had built, but in the end neither party could come up with a price or setup that made sense to the other. We thought he was interested in a licensing deal where we continued to invest in the brand (with stories and such). But he wanted to take over the brand as it was and apply it to a variety or related products purchased and resold from China. Being that our personal brands were so closely tied to TROBO brand, we couldn't see a great way to make that work. So we declined.

That holiday season we sold out the remaining units of TROBO robots. The following year, we kept the store open. Chris had some ideas he was still interested in pursuing and ended up publishing a first chapter reader targeted at 5-6 year olds. It was intended to be the first of a series that introduced the TROBOs world, where they come from, what they learn as children, etc. but with both of us being back to full time jobs, there was zero marketing of the book. We just didn't find the energy or time.

When you fail, you learn. We spent a lot of time that year reflecting on the financial failure and what we could have done differently. We recognized two lessons that we'll pass along to entrepreneurs. **On a macro level, these two lessons may be the most significant hindsight lessons in this book and our journey.**

First, the major thing we really misunderstood as founders is something young entrepreneurs should strive to do better than we did; it is critical to understand your business model and generate financial proformas as soon as humanly possible. These two go hand in hand. *On a related note, the Lean Startup methodology only promotes basic business modeling and doesn't teach anything about financially understanding your business. As a result, it gives a false sense of security when you complete it.* These days we see this gaping knowledge hole in almost all startup teams we mentor. Founders don't know the how the business model they are getting into works, specifically around sales cycles, and they don't realize they are missing key team members (often a proven sales person or partner who actually knows the industry they are entering). Often the founding team has the technical person, maybe an operations person, or way too many techs and not enough of the other types. Most of them have never generated a financial proforma and have no idea of the importance of modeling their businesses. Young entrepreneurs who really think this through early can make stronger choices in direction on where they take their company or could choose to stop progress on one idea altogether in favor of another.

Second, Geoffrey A. Moore's book, Crossing the Chasm, discusses the struggle entrepreneurs have in taking their product from "early stage" adopters to the "early majority" (or mass market for us). We had successfully found our early stage market with Kickstarter-type customers. They were willing to buy and promote TROBO to like-minded customers. We had achieved acceptable sales and delivered on all our commitments to early customers. That part of our model worked very well. Though what we were doing (including selling in low volumes on Amazon and directly on our site) was acceptable for that stage it was not scalable.

Making the leap also involves *scaling*. Unfortunately we weren't ready to make the leap across the chasm. The leap would have entailed getting the price, product, packaging, and promotion (the 4 Ps of Marketing) to the mix that the mass market customer would want to purchase it, regardless of whether they knew or cared about who we were. The mass market customer wants a product that comes in at a price point only achievable with mass manufactured volumes. They want lots of content. They have certain price expectations for plush toys. The viewership of Shark

Tank IS the mass market. So the lesson here is that essentially when you go on Shark Tank, you need to be ready for the leap or you need to have already made it. The viewership is in that mindset, and really even the show's investors are in that mindset. If the mix is not correct, you'll struggle to get a deal and you'll struggle to make sales. If we had been ready for the late adopters with the right marketing mix of the 4Ps, we might have been successful with the airing of the episode. With the right marketing mix, our business model would have been working to the point where the other investors we met would have readily invested. We weren't ready to scale, so they weren't ready to invest. Without an investor to help us reach production scales necessary to get the right mix, we could not make the leap. It is a chicken and egg kind of thing sometimes. And without enough financial runway to understand that, fix it, react, and then become ready for mass adoption or investment for scale, we just hit the ceiling and fell into the metaphorical chasm that Geoffrey describes in his book. It was a long, slow fall, but it happened none the less. Regardless of whether you get the opportunity to go on a show like Shark Tank, new entrepreneurs need to know they must plan enough time into their efforts to push for that leap. Knowing doesn't make it any easier, but you should still have a plan to try.

After one year of being open to support existing customers and explore any last chance opportunities, we closed the company right at the beginning of 2018. We officially shut down the site that following May and made the app stories and games free to use.

Emotions: When an Entrepreneur has to close their business, it can be devastating. In our experience, it was slow, painful, somewhat surreal, and sometimes now when we look back on it, it almost feels like a dream.

Lessons: Know your business model inside and out; the sooner the better. Know what you will be good at when entering a business and know what you will need to learn a lot about (or get more team members to help fill in the gaps). Having gone through Kickstarter, getting an SBIR grant, getting into Amazon Exclusives, Tech Crunch, and even getting on Shark Tank among many other things, it seems like all the right checkboxes were in place from a marketing aspect, and we often get complimented on how well we built the brand. But all the best marketing in the world and having a well developed product can't help you, if you can't get your business model to make the leap across whatever your chasm looks like.

Life After TROBO

At the time of this writing, Jeremy is part of an experience innovation team at Universal Parks & Resorts, and Chris is a VP of Engineering at a company with recent VC investment and high growth potential. Our children and families are well. Although TROBO did not turn out to be a financial success, we still both learned more about running a business, what we don't know, and further defined what our strengths and weaknesses are. We're grateful for having taken the adventure, and we'd do it again, although a bit differently the second time around for sure. TROBO will always hold a special place in our hearts and minds and in those of our families. We hope you have enjoyed this journey with us.

Special Thanks

As we have mentioned in our story, it takes a village to build a robot. We are grateful to all of those people who are listed below (listed roughly in alphabetical order) and our apologies to those who we may have accidentally left out (there were so many helping us make TROBO a success, just know we care):

All of our Kickstarter Backers
Steve & Linda Alcorn
Bess Auer

Jean Bastien
Ron Ben Zeev
Terry Brennan
George Boraiko
Jon Capriola
Kirstie Chadwick
Orrett Davis
Carlos Donze
Deirdre Englehart, EdD
FIEA, our FIEA Grads, and our Writers
David Glass
Michael Grysikiewicz
Jack Henkel
Shanti Hill
Dr. Atsusi Hirumi
Phillip Holt
Michael Judith
David Judy
Laura Kern
Alan Kirk
Michael Kramer
Dr. Glenn Larsen
Judith and Moshe Mann
Professor Josh Murdock
Gregg Pollack
Necole Pynn
Shahier Rahman
The Real Visualz team

Rob Richardson
Mark Burginger
Bruce and Susan Scheinberg
Shark Tank and ABC
Roger Shiffman
The Starter Studio gang
Donna Mackenzie
The Firespring Fund team
Cora and Bill Sterling
Meir and Melissa Wasserman

Our early Vendors that cut us a break
Our Parental Focus Group members
All of the News Reporters and Bloggers that showed us love

And most of all, we would like to thank our wives – Laurie and Rachel – and our children – Sophia, Jacob and Asher – for all of their love, understanding and support that has kept us going.

Jeremy and Chris

www.ingramcontent.com/pod-product-compliance
Lightning Source LLC
Chambersburg PA
CBHW060621210326
41520CB00010B/1424